SCHOOL ESSAYS, PARAGRAPHS, LETTERS, COMPREHENSION AND STORIES

[FOR PRIMARY CLASSES]

By

MADAN SOOD MA

(Formerly of Indian Air Force)

GOODWILL PUBLISHING HOUSE®

B-3 RATTAN JYOTI, 18 RAJENDRA PLACE

NEW DELHI -110008 (INDIA)

Published by
GOODWILL PUBLISHING HOUSE®
B-3 Rattan Jyoti, 18 Rajendra Place
New Delhi-110008 (INDIA)
Tel : 25750801, 25820556
Fax : 91-11-25764396
E-mail : goodwillpub@vsnl.net
Website : www.goodwillpublishinghouse.com

PREFACE

This book encompasses a wide range of essays, paragraphs, stories, letters and comprehension and is meant for students studying at Primary level. There are variegated themes to motivate the learner to use English for purpose of communication and expression. A conscious effort has been made to provide interesting reading material. The book aims at facilitating extra reading, for students of all standards are expected to read beyond the prescribed text books.

All categories of essays, paragraphs, stories and letters find a place in this book. The Introduction Section provides a comprehensive background to the learners about the topics that have been dealt in the book. As the comprehension of the given passage and to provide answers to the questions asked pertaining to the passage form part of all tests/examinations from Primary to the highest level examinations, exercises on comprehension will enable the students to solve any unseen passage which they may come across in their school tests or annual examinations.

Includes very useful exercises on Practical Grammar/ Usage and answers to fully solved exercises have been provided to enable the students to evaluate their grasp of the topics.

MADAN SOOD

CONTENTS

SECTION 1

INTRODUCTION

ESSAY WRITING

The word 'essay' literally means an attempt and an essay is an exercise in composition wherein you are to express your thoughts in good English. Precisely speaking, it is a written composition giving expression to one's own personal ideas on some topic.

Characteristics of a Good Essay

1. **Unity** : An essay must develop one thought with a definite purpose and the subject should be clearly defined in the mind and kept in view throughout.

2. **Order** : The essay should follow a certain order and come to a definite conclusion.

3. **Brevity** : An essay, especially a school essay, should not be long and it should be a brief exercise, concisely expressed.

4. **Style** : The style of an essay must be dignified and literary. Slang terms and free and easy constructions should be avoided.

5. **Personal touch** : An essay should express the personal feelings and ideas of the writer, as an essay is a written composition giving expression to personal ideas or opinions on a subject.

Hints on Essay Writing

If one wants to write good essays, one must acquire the habit of reading. As all knowledge does not come from books, we should observe and learn much from the life around us. We can also improve the skill of writing essays by conversing with others.

You should have a clear and accurate conception of the subject of the essay before you attempt to write on it.

This should be followed by collecting material for your essay before you can write it. All essays should be divided into paragraphs.

Structure of an Essay should have three parts — the Introduction, the Body of the Essay and the Conclusion.

PARAGRAPHS

Chapters, Essays and other prose compositions are broken up into paragraphs to make their meaning easier. A number of sentences grouped together and relating to one topic or a group of related sentences that develop a single point or idea is called a paragraph.

Paragraphs may be short or long. A paragraph may consist of a single sentence or many sentences.

Essentials of a Paragraph

1. **Unity** : Every sentence in the paragraph must be closely connected with the main topic of the paragraph. The paragraph and every part of it must express one theme or topic.

2. **Order** : Events must be related in the order of their occurrence and all ideas should be connected with the leading idea and arranged according to their importance of order.

3. **Variety :** In order to avoid monotony, the paragraphs of a composition should be of different lengths and not always of the same sentence construction.

STORIES

To write a good story, one must have the whole plot clear in one's mind. The main points should be arranged in their proper order. While writing a story, important items should not be omitted. The leading points should be emphasised. One should not dwell too long on minor details and should not repeat oneself.

LETTERS

There are several different kinds of letters. There are certain formats which apply to all the letters. They are explained below :

1. Heading, consisting of (a) the writer's address, (b) the date
2. Salutation
3. The body of the letter
4. The courteous leave-taking or conclusion
5. The signature
6. The superscription on the envelope.

1. **The Heading :** The heading informs the reader where and when the letter was written. The *where* is the writer's full postal address and the *when* gives the date on which the letter was written.

2. **Salutation :**

(i) To members of one's family :

My dear Mother
Dear Mother
Dear Father

My dear Father
Dear Uncle

(ii) To friends :
Dear Rakesh
Dear Sohan etc.

3. Body of the letter

1. Letter should be divided into paragraphs unless it is very short.
2. The language of the letter should be simple and direct.
3. Think out what you want to say and before you start writing the letter, put down your points in some logical order.
4. Commas, full stops and semi colons should be put in their proper places.

Leave-taking phrase must be written below the last words of the letter and to the left side of the page.

Note : The first word of subscription must begin with a capital letter; e.g., Sincerely yours

COMPREHENSION

1. The passage should be read fairly quickly.

2. This should be followed by a second reading, a little slowly, to know the details.

3. Now study the questions thoroughly and turn to the relevant portions of the passage.

4. Read them again and then rewrite them in your own words.

5. Do not pick up the original language. Write in your own style using your own words.

6. If meanings of any words or phrases are to be given, care should be taken to use the same part of speech.

SECTION 2

ESSAYS

1. My Best Friend

A true friend is a gift from God. Everyone has some friends. I also have many friends. But Rajesh is my best friend. He is my class fellow. His father is a doctor. His mother is a teacher. He is an obedient boy. He is very good in studies. All the teachers like him. He helps the students who are weak in studies. He is very punctual. He never comes late to school. He is a good sportsman. He is tall and healthy. He is the captain of our cricket team. He is kind, gentle and courteous. He respects all his elders. He never gets angry. He hates no body. I feel very happy in his company. I am proud of my friend. ●

2. My House

I live in Shanti Niketan. It is a beautiful colony in South Delhi. My house is situated in Street No. 2. My father built this house in 1998. We are a family of five members — my grand father, my father, my mother and my sister. My house has three bedrooms and a drawing-cum-dining room.

In the front of my house, there is a beautiful lawn. In the backyard, there is a small vegetable garden. There is a sofa set, a dining table and a T.V. set in the drawing room. In the centre, there is a carpet. There are some beautiful paintings on the walls.

There is a kitchen, a bathroom and a store house in our house. We have a gas stove. The crockery is kept neatly on the shelves. I like my house very much. ●

3. My Hobby or How I Spend My Spare Time or The Pastime I Like

Different people have different hobbies. Hobbies keep us busy and happy. My hobby is gardening. Whenever I have spare time, I go to my small garden. I see the little plants grow. I water them. I sow seeds in the vacant space and water them. I take care of them. I have also grown many flowers. They give me great joy.

I work with a spade and hoe every morning and evening in my small garden. I root out the unwanted plants. There is a banana plant also in my garden. There are other types of fruit tree as well. I grow some vegetables also in my garden. I feel very happy to see the fruits, plants and flowers in my garden. My hobby gives me a lot of exercise as well. ●

4. My First Day at School

My father wanted me to join a school. He got me admitted to my school on an auspicious day. My mother blessed me. I carried a bag and went to school with my father. We went to the office of the Principal. I was a little afraid. My father filled up a form. I was taken to the Ist class of the Primary Section. My class teacher received me. He was very polite. My father had carried sweets. My class teacher distributed the sweets among the children and teachers. Then my father left me in the school.

A boy read out the lesson. All of us began repeating it. I could not learn much on the first day. The last bell rang. I went home with my father. ●

5. My Neighbour

A good neighbour is a blessing. Good neighbours can help one another. Sohan is my next-door neighbour. He is not a rich man. He works hard to earn his bread. He has a small family. He is happy with his lot. Everyone respects him in our neighbourhood. He wears a simple dress. His children also live a simple life. He has got a good health. All the members of his family work hard.

He is always ready to serve and help his neighbours. He is a selfless person. He never expects favours from others. He earns through the sweat of his brow but he never complains. We are very lucky to have a good neighbour. ●

6. My Class Teacher
or
My Best Teacher
or
The Ideal Teacher

Mr. Rajnish Sharma is my class teacher. He is M.A. B.Ed. He is very popular among students. He teaches us English. He is like a friend and guide to the students. He maintains discipline in the class. He is very polite. He is strict with those who break discipline. Everyone in the school loves and respects him.

He does his duty honestly. He takes pains to explain the lessons. He gives us moral lessons. He joins us in

games. He guides us in every possible way. He leads a simple life. He is a man of noble ideals.

He advises us in every moment of difficulty. He follows the principles of truth, non-violence and courtesy. He is master of his subject. His English pronunciation is very impressive. He teaches grammar very well. I like him very much.

7. My Pet Animal
or
The Animal I Like Most
or
My Faithful Dog

I have got a dog. Its colour is white. There are brown patches on its body. It can smell any danger. As soon as I return home, it wags its tail to welcome me. If I am late to come home, it waits for me on the roadside. It barks at strangers. It shows love and respect to the guests and welcomes visitors.

My younger brother and sister are fond of my dog. They play with it. It shows love to them. It goes along with me in the morning. It follows me to the nearby garden. It wanders about in the plants.

My dog guards the house like a watchman. It is a faithful companion. It is very bold. It takes risks to guard our house. I am very fond of my dog.

8. My School

I study in S.D. School Moti Bagh. It is situated in South Delhi. It is an ideal school. My school has a big and spacious building. It is a double-storeyed building. It has forty classrooms. The rooms are well-ventilated and well-furnished. My school has a big library. There are about fifteen thousand books in the library.

The Principal of my school is a very good administrator. He always tries his best to improve the school. All the teachers in my school are hard-working. The result of the school is always good. The Principal is very interested in sports and games. My school has a big playground. We play different games in the playground.

The laboratories are well-equipped. Students take part in various curricular activities. I like my school very much. ●

9. My School Library

My school library is housed in a big room. The room is well-furnished. It is airy. About seventy students can sit in the library. The books are arranged in almirahs. There are books on Science, Geography, History, Economics, Political Science, Sociology and Literature. There is a large number of children's books.

Magazines and journals are kept on the tables. The titles of the books are displayed on boards. My school library is a quiet place. It remains open all day.

Mr. Suresh Ahluwalia is the librarian. He is an intelligent person. He keeps the books in proper order.

Students can read and borrow all types of books. He helps the students to choose good books.

The library is a very useful place in the school. ●

10. A Railway Journey

During the last summer vacation, I went to Shimla. I travelled by train with my mother.

We packed our luggage and hired an auto-rikshaw. We reached the railway station. We bought tickets and then returned to the platform. There was a big crowd of people waiting for the train. Some people were standing and some others were sitting on the benches.

The train arrived. We entered our compartment. We had comfortable seats near the windows. There were people of different States and different areas in the train. Some passengers were polite and some were rude. Some were talkative and others were quiet.

The train started. I started looking out of the window. Green fields looked very beautiful. After six hours we reached Kalka station. We had dinner at the platform. We again got in the train. The small engine ran on the narrow rail tracks.

I enjoyed the scenery of green hills on either side of the railway line. We also passed through the dark tunnels. The journey to Shimla was very pleasant. ●

11. A Journey by Bus

Once I travelled by bus from Delhi to Jaipur. I reached the bus stand. I got a ticket. The bus started after half an hour at 6 p.m. It travelled at a good speed although there was a lot of traffic on the way.

The lorries, buses, cars and other vehicles passed on the way. Soon dusk fell. There was darkness everywhere. There were road lights near the towns. Suddenly, the bus stopped. There was some trouble in the engine.

It was very cold at night. There were about fifty passengers who were travelling with us. The driver came out of the bus. He took the help of another bus driver. They opened the engine and did some adjustments.

Fortunately, the bus started again. I reached Jaipur one hour late. There was no mishap on the way. ●

12. An Indian Festival — Diwali

Diwali is a very famous festival. It is celebrated in honour of Lord Rama. On this day Lord Rama returned to Ayodhya after fourteen years of exile.

People make great preparations to celebrate this festival. They whitewash their houses. They purchase earthen lamps and candles to illuminate their houses. Bulbs of different colours are also used. The sweet-sellers prepare sweets. The shop-keepers display their goods.

People wear fine clothes. They enjoy the occasion. They purchase sweets and offer gifts and sweets to their friends and relations. Sugar toys are also sold. The rows of burning candles and lamps present a beautiful sight. Many people buy new utensils.

At night people worship the goddess Lakshmi. She is the goddess of wealth. Some people gamble on this day. It is a bad habit. Children enjoy Diwali by bursting crackers. ●

13. My Favourite Leader or A Great Indian Leader

Mahatma Gandhi is my favourite leader. He is called the Father of the Nation. He raised his voice against the British rulers. India got freedom under his leadership.

He was born on October 2, 1869 at Porbandar in Gujarat. His father was the Diwan of Rajkot. His mother's name was Putlibai. He got his early education at Rajkot. After passing his matriculation, he went to England for higher studies.

He returned from England as a lawyer. He then went to South Africa. In South Africa he worked to improve the condition of Indians living there. He returned to India and took part in the Indian Freedom Movement.

Truth and non-violence were his great weapons. He worked to remove poverty, economic inequality and untouchability. After Independence, he worked for Hindu-Muslim unity. On 30th January 1948, he was shot dead by Nathu Ram Godse. ●

14. A Scene at a Railway Station

A railway station is a very busy place. Yesterday I went to New Delhi Railway Station to receive my uncle. I went by bus. There was a great rush outside the railway station. Taxis, buses and scooters were parked outside. There were people of all ages outside the ticket window. There were long queues. I bought a platform ticket and went inside.

A large number of men, women and children were waiting for the train. Some were sitting on the benches. There was an announcement. The train was late by one hour. It was difficult to pass the time.

I went to the tea stall and had a cup of tea. Then I went to the bookstall. I bought a magazine. Other people were also buying books and magazines. Then I took a round of the platform. The coolies were moving about carrying luggage on their head.

The train arrived. The passengers rushed to board the train. Many passengers came out of the compartment. I received my uncle. We went home by an auto-rickshaw. ●

15. Your Neighbour or A Good Neighbour

I live in Karol Bagh. It is a crowded part of the city. We have neighbours of all kinds. They are of different castes and religions. Mr. Kailash is my next door neighbour. He is a businessman. He deals in ready-made garments. He has one son and one daughter. His son is of my age. He is my class fellow. Mr. Kailash is a popular person. He is soft-spoken. He is cultured and polite. There is always a smile on his face.

He is very cooperative by nature. He is not very rich. But he always helps the needy persons. His wife also is a very kind lady. She is well-educated. Whenever we have any problem, she comes to our help. There are other neighbours too. But Mr. Kailash is my best neighbour. ●

16. A Scene at the Bus Stop

A bus stop is an interesting place. There are always passengers at the bus stops. During the peak hours there is a huge rush at the bus stops. I go to my school by bus.

Yesterday I reached the bus stop a little earlier than usual. There was a great rush at the stop. Some people were standing in a queue. Some people were standing all around. Everyone was in a hurry.

Some people were talking. Some were reading newspapers. Some were discussing politics. Some were discussing about the law and order problem, while others were discussing about the rising prices.

As soon as the bus arrived, all the passengers ran to board it. There was pushing and pulling. The queue was broken. I could not get into the bus. The bus took a few passengers and moved on.

After sometime another bus on the same route came. It was also packed. Somehow, I was able to get inside the bus. There was no place even to stand properly.

I got down after four stands. I have to face this problem everyday. Buses are always overcrowded during peak time. ●

17. A Visit to a Zoo

A visit to a zoo is an interesting experience. Last Sunday I went to Delhi zoo with my father. We went there by bus. Delhi zoo is near Purana Quila.

My father bought the tickets and we entered the gate. There were ponds on both the sides of the road. Ducks were swimming in the ponds. We saw kangaroos, elephants, stags, deer and 'Neelgai' etc. I saw a young kangaroo in his mother's skin pouch.

Then we came to the cages of birds. There were different kinds of birds. Peacocks were in large numbers. Then we saw the tigers in their enclosures. We also saw monkeys, chimpanzees and apes.

Then we saw rhinos and giraffes. After going round the zoo, we came out and sat under a tree. We had our food which we had carried with us. We returned home tired but very happy. ●

18. A Visit to an Exhibition

The 2nd Industrial Trade Fair was held in Pragati Maidan on Mathura Road. It was organised by the Small Scale Industries Department. Every State of India had decorated its stall. A large number of people came to see the fair.

I went to see this fair with my friend last week. There was a large crowd of people outside the gate. We bought tickets and entered the exhibition grounds. The pavilions of Delhi, Rajasthan, Karnataka and Uttar Pradesh were very attractive.

Japan, China and Canada had also set up beautiful pavilions. We saw the industrial progress of these countries. The toys of Japan were liked very much by the children. There was a toy train for the children.

In the States' pavilions, the industrialists and businessmen were busy in finalising business deals. The craftsmen were showing their skills. We learnt a lot from this fair. We enjoyed the fair and returned home. ●

19. A Visit to a Village Fair

Fairs and festivals are held in every town and village of India. The people living in villages have no entertainment except the fairs.

I went to see a village fair with my friend. There were many men, women and children going to see the fair.

They were wearing colourful clothes. They came from the neighbouring villages.

First of all, the people worshipped the goddess in the Kali temple. They placed the offerings of sweets in front of the goddess.

There was a great hustle and bustle in the markets. There were many shops in a row. There were shops of bangles, ready-made garments, toys and sweets. A flute-seller was playing on his flute. The children were enjoying rides on the merry-go-round. There were also rope-dancers and magicians. The snake charmers and jugglers were also there. There were some policemen who were maintaining law and order in the fair.

A small boy had separated from his parents. He was given to his parents by the scouts. When it became dark and we returned to our homes. It was a very happy visit.

●

20. Recess Period in Your School

The recess period is very exciting. The school bell goes for the lunch break. There is a great noise in the whole building. The children rush out of their classrooms. They wait for this period impatiently.

Most of the students take their lunch boxes and sit in the playground. They sit in groups of three or four. They take their food and rush to the water taps.

There is a great rush at the school canteen. Some students play different games in the play ground. Some students go to the library. They read newspapers and magazines. Some students sit in their classrooms. They complete their homework. They do not play or buy anything from the canteen. The teachers sit in the staff room. Some teachers take some food or tea. They refresh themselves for the remaining periods.

When the bell goes, all the children go back to their classrooms. ●

21. A Morning Walk

Nature is at her best in the morning. This time is very pleasant. I go for a morning walk regularly. I go to a park. This park is just a short distance away from my house.

In the morning, the air is cool and very fresh. The birds sing happily. The peacocks dance in the fields. There are dew drops on the green grass.

The fresh air in the park refreshes my mind and body. I walk bare-foot on the grass. Morning walk gives me health and happiness. I feel energetic for the whole day. Morning walk keeps me away from sickness. Morning walk is a very good exercise. It purifies my blood. I enjoy the morning walk very much. ●

22. The Picnic I Enjoyed Most
or
An Outing

Last Sunday I made a programme to go on a picnic with my friends. We went to Okhla. The weather was very fine. We went by bus. We reached Okhla at 9 a.m. We went to the park near the power house. There we spread our rugs under the shady trees.

It was a beautiful place. Many people had come there for a picnic. Men, women and children were playing there. Some were enjoying boating. Some students were busy in fishing. We took a joy ride on the camel. We also had a dip in the cold water. Some of us swam and dived in the cold water.

Then we had our lunch which we had carried with us. We played games for some more time. It began to grow dark. We decided to return home. We came back at 7 p.m. It was a wonderful day. ●

23. A Rainy Day

Rain is both a blessing and a curse. Sometimes we like rains but sometimes we do not like them.

Last week I went to my uncle's house in Green Park. There was no wind. It was a pleasant day. It was not very hot. All of a sudden, it became dark. Clouds appeared in the sky. As I got into the bus, it started raining. It was a very heavy downpour. Soon the roads were flooded. Traffic came to a standstill.

I got down from the bus. Soon I was fully drenched. There was water everywhere. It started entering the low lying shops. Benches and chairs began to float in the water. The people started running to protect themselves from the rain. The people inside the buses too got wet.

It rained continuously for two hours. All activities came to a standstill. The rain caused water logging everywhere. The roads were damaged due to the heavy and continuous rain. ●

24. Advantages and Disadvantages of Science

Modern age is the age of science. The world has become smaller. The railway engine has replaced the bullock cart. The aeroplane takes us to distant places in a few hours. Man can fly at a speed of more than 2000 kilometres per hour. Man has reached the moon the with the help of science.

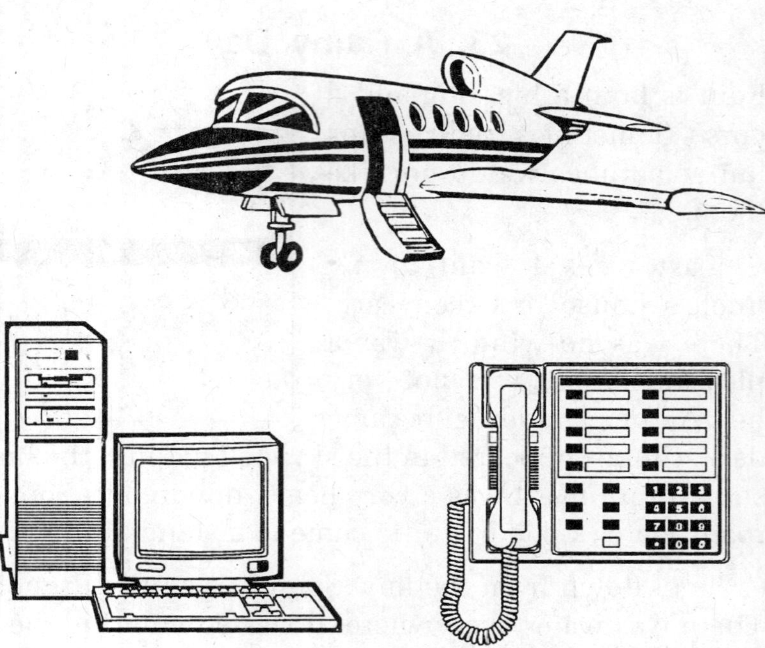

Science has changed our domestic life. Electricity is used in place of coal. We cook on gas stoves. Computers, televisions and radios have made life more pleasant. Heaters, irons, washing machines, freezers, and room-coolers are in common use.

We can talk on the mobile phone at a distance of thousands of kilometres. Everything is made with the help of machines. The cost of production has gone down. Farmers use many machines in agriculture. Chemicals are used in the fields. In the field of medicine and surgery, science has made wonderful progress.

But science has also produced many destructive weapons. It has given atom bombs, hydrogen bombs, tanks, missiles etc. in the hands of man. It has raised the threat of a nuclear war. Science can be man's friend as well as enemy. ●

25. My Choice of a Profession or My Aim in Life or My Ambition in Life

Different people have different ambitions. Some wish to become rich. Some people want to get a high rank or position.

My father is not a rich man. He can not spend much money for Medical or Engineering courses. Therefore I have decided to become a teacher. A teacher's profession is a noble profession. He is a nation builder. A teacher can change the fortune of his students.

I shall take personal interest in the future of my students. I shall keep my knowledge up to the mark. I will try to solve all the difficulties of my students. I shall take interest in my work. I shall try to be an ideal teacher. I have chosen this ambition with confidence and after a lot of thinking. ●

26. A House on Fire

Yesterday evening I was doing my home work in my room. Suddenly, I heard a noise in the street. I at once rushed outside. The people were crying 'Fire' ! 'Fire' !

A house in the next street was on fire. People were throwing water on the fire. I also joined them. Some people were throwing dust and sand on the fire.

The fire was spreading fast. A child was left inside the house. A young boy jumped into the house and took out the crying child. Everybody praised the courage and brave action of the young boy.

Soon the fire brigade arrived. The fire men fought the flames bravely. They threw water on the rising flames. It took two hours to control the fire. The whole house was reduced to ashes. Fortunately, there was no loss of life. ●

27. A Visit to a Hill Station

We decided to go to Kashmir during the summer vacation. I went there with my parents. We left for Jammu by train. We reached Jammu the following morning. We stayed in Jammu for one day. Then we went to Srinagar by bus.

We saw Shalimar Bagh and Nishat Garden. There were very beautiful flowers and fruit trees in the garden. I enjoyed the beauty of Nature. We hired a 'Shikara' in Dal lake. We also went to see Gulmarg. It is very famous for its beauty.

Then we went to Pahalgam. It is also a very beautiful place. Kashmir is famous for its handicrafts. We bought some wooden toys, sarees and shawls.

We stayed in Kashmir for ten days. Then we returned to Delhi. The sweet memory of the Kashmir Valley is still fresh in my mind. ●

28. The City I Live In

I live in Delhi. It is the capital of India. Delhi is a centre of trade and commerce. It is a historical city. It has many beautiful monuments. The Red Fort and Jama Masjid were built by Shahajahan. They are in Old Delhi. The Qutab Minar, the Old Fort, Humayun's Tomb, Safdarjung's Tomb, Jantar Mantar etc. are old monuments. A large number of people visit these places everyday.

The Parliament House and India Gate are the new buildings. Delhi is a great centre of education. There are many universities and colleges in Delhi. Students come from different parts of the world to study here.

Delhi has some very famous shopping centres like Chandni Chowk, Karol Bagh, Connaught Place, Ansal Plaza, Palika Bazaar etc. There are many five-star hotels in Delhi.

Air pollution, water pollution and noise pollution have increased in Delhi. But the government is trying to solve this problem. ●

29. A Visit to a Circus Show

Last Sunday, I went to see a circus show with my friends. The circus party was called Great Gemini Circus.

We reached there at 6.30 p.m. There was a great rush. We bought tickets and went in. The tent was decorated with colourful lights. The seating arrangement was good. First of all, a group of young boys and girls came on the stage. They welcomed the visitors. Then there was a ladder show. A girl climbed up the ladder without any support. Another girl came on a cycle with one wheel.

Then the jokers came. It was great fun. A ring master came with a lion. The lion obeyed him. Then monkeys and elephants showed different feats of skill. A young girl showed her shooting skill. The elephant saluted the people with its trunk. The horses came and ran in a circle. It was a very interesting show. All enjoyed it. ●

30. A Road Accident

Road accidents are a common feature of big cities. Rash driving causes accidents. Some drivers do not obey the traffic rules.

Last Sunday, there was an accident near India Gate. A car was coming at a very high speed. One cyclist was coming from the opposite direction. The car hit the cyclist while taking a turn. Another car collided with this car. The cyclist fell down. His head struck against the ground.

He became senseless. The car driver tried to escape. But the people caught him. They handed him to the police. The wounded cyclist was removed to the hospital.

We can avoid road accidents if we obey traffic rules. We should not drive our vehicles very fast.

31. A Visit to a Historical Building
or
A Visit to the Red Fort

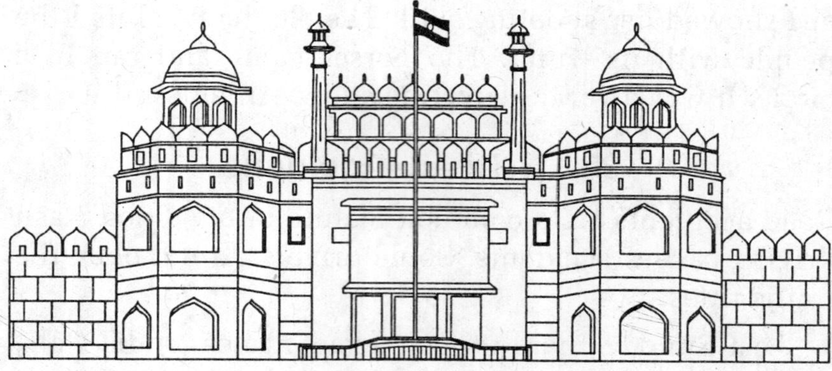

Delhi is a historical city. Many historical buildings were built in Delhi during the rule of Emperor Shahjahan.

Last Sunday I went to see the Red Fort with my uncle and cousins. They had arrived from a village.

We bought tickets and entered a big gate. This gate is called Lahori Gate. Many people had come to see the

Red Fort. We passed through a beautiful market. First of all, we saw Diwan-i-Aam. It is made of red sandstone. The roof of Diwan-i-Aam is supported by a large number of columns and arches. Here Emperor Shahjahan used to sit on the Peacock throne.

Then we saw Diwan-i-Khas. Royal palaces are in front of Diwan-i-Khas. The palaces are made of pure white marble. A canal runs through these palaces.

We also saw Moti Masjid and Savan and Bhadon Houses. This building is a fine example of architecture. The beauty in the marble is worth-seeing. We spent two hours in the Red Fort and then we returned home. ●

32. Advantages and Disadvantages of Examinations

Examinations are held in every school or college. They are the test of learning. There are defects in the present examination system. But exams are needed to test the knowledge.

Both the bright and weak students fear examinations. A student may not like examination but he has to face it every year. Therefore, he should prepare notes regularly at home. He should devote time to every subject. There is a choice in the question paper. If a student prepares well, he gets good marks. Good marks give fruit in the future.

Examination is like a fever. If a student is nervous, he can not learn anything. Examinations are not a true test of a student's ability. They are the test of cramming, not of knowledge.

It is not possible to test in three hours what a student has learnt during the whole year. Some students copy in the examination. They tear leaves from the books.

Thus, examinations are not the true test of one's ability but there is no other way of testing the ability of a student. Examinations cannot thus be removed. ●

33. A Bank Robbery or A Burglary in Your Neighbourhood

Crimes in big cities like Delhi are increasing day by day. Last Wednesday a burglary took place in the Punjab National Bank in Punjabi Bagh.

The bank was crowded with customers. Two robbers having fire-arms entered the bank. They pushed the customers to one corner. One of the robbers raised his gun and asked the cashier to hand over the currency notes. All were scared. Two robbers were standing at the gate. One of the robbers put the currency notes in two big bags.

The cashier tried to snatch the bags but he could. One of the robbers fired in the air. The manager pressed the alarm bell. The robbers rushed out and got into the car which was already parked near the bank.

The Police arrived and chased the robbers but it was too late. The car, used by the robbers, was found by the police later in a deserted place. ●

34. A Visit to a Village

Last week I visited my village. My father is in the Army. He left his village when he was nineteen years old. Since then we had never visited the place. My uncle had invited me to visit our village.

My village is near Saharanpur. I went to Saharanpur by train. From there I took a bus. It is five kilometres from Saharanpur. My uncle was waiting for me at the road side.

I met my aunt and other members of the family. It was a hot day. I took a bath at the farm well. I bathed in the open for the first time. I enjoyed the cold water very much. Then I went to the mango orchard. There I plucked mangoes with my own hands. Then I took lunch. It was a very simple meal of maize flour bread, curd and vegetables.

In the evening I visited the farm. My uncle was watering the crops. I milked the cow for the first time in my life. I lived in the village for fifteen days. When I returned, many people came to see me off. I was very impressed by the simple living of the village people. ●

35. Our School Peon

Peon is a very important person in a school. Sohan Lal is the peon of our school. He is a very good man. All the teachers and students like him.

Sohan Lal is about twenty six years old. He has passed his Middle School Examination. He wears the school uniform when he is on duty. He is a hard-working man. He reaches the school before the school starts. He opens the rooms. He dusts the Principal's office and the Staff Room. He is sincere and regular in his work.

He sits outside the Principal's room. He takes the letters and other circulars from the Principal to the teachers. He can read and write Hindi and English. He keeps the school Notice Board up-to-date.

All the teachers like him and praise him for his work. He is preparing for the Matriculation examination. He takes help from the teachers. He lives in the school. He rings the bell in time. He keeps the class registers at the proper place. He works very hard but his pay is less. ●

36. The Marriage of My Brother
or
The Wedding you have Attended

My elder brother's marriage was fixed for ninth April. There was great excitement. The preparations were made many days in advance.

Wedding cards were sent to relatives and friends. They started arriving a few days before the wedding day. Ornaments, sarees etc. were purchased. The marriage procession started at 7 p.m. The marriage party was to go to Rohini.

The band was playing. The bridegroom was riding a white mare. All the people were wearing beautiful dresses. The procession reached the bride's house at 10 p.m.

The marriage party was welcomed. Garlands were offered. Then the delicious dishes were served. At night the *pandits* performed the wedding ceremony. We left the bride's house in the morning along with the *doli*. The reception ceremony was held the next day. ●

37. The Life of a Farmer

A farmer lives in a village. He has a farm. He grows food crops. He gets up early in the morning. He prepares fodder for the animals. Then he milks his cows. He then goes to the fields.

He ploughs the fields. He waters them. The routine of the farmer is never disturbed by sun or rain, cold or heat. He stays on the farm till the evening. He takes lunch on the farm. Then he takes rest for some time under a shady tree.

In the evening he returns home. He brings his cattle with him. He takes his dinner and then sleeps. Sometimes he goes to the *chopal* or the village square to discuss the village matters. ●

38. Prize Distribution Function in Our School or Annual Day Celebrations in Our School

The Annual Day celebrations were held in our school on 3rd October. The Lt. Governor was the chief guest. He gave away the prizes.

Preparations were made many days in advance. The school building was white washed. Then it was decorated. The *pandal* was decorated. Chairs were arranged for the parents and other guests. The gate was decorated with flowers, balloons and buntings. The function started at 5 p.m.

The chief guest arrived on time. The N.C.C. cadets and the scouts gave a salute to the chief guest. Some students showed the gymnastic exercises. Then the cultural programme started.

A drama was staged. Action songs were sung. The Principal read out the annual report. The chief guest gave away the prizes. He congratulated the Principal and the staff on the progress made by the school. The function came to an end at 9 p.m. with the singing of the National Anthem. ●

39. If I were the Prime Minister of India

If I were the Prime Minister of India, I would make India a strong country. I would try to make Indian forces the most powerful in the world. I would like to remove poverty and unemployment from India.

I would take steps for the improvement of agriculture if I were the Prime Minister of India. I would give old age pension and unemployment allowance to the needy persons. I would set up small-scale industries in different parts of the country. I would control the black-marketing and hoarding of essential commodities.

I would establish peace with the neighbouring countries. I would create an atmosphere of friendship all over the country. ●

40. A Cricket Match

Last Sunday a cricket match was played between our school team and the team of S.D. School. The match was played in the playgrounds of our school. It was a very interesting match. Mr. Rakesh Sharma and Rajneesh Katiyar were the umpires. The match started at 9 a.m.

Our captain won the toss. He decided to bat first. The opening batsmen of our team batted very well. They made 107 runs. Our players were out after scoring 213 runs.

S.D. School did not start well. Three wickets fell for 36 runs. We were happy. We were hopeful of our victory. But due to the 6th wicket partnership, their score reached 208 runs. We were quite tense.

The one after the other S.D. School lost all their wickets. They could score only 210 runs. So we won the exciting match by 3 runs. ●

41. Newspapers

Newspapers are found all over the world. They are published in many languages. We get newspapers early in the morning. They are useful because they tell us about the world.

Newspapers give us information about our country. The latest events are published in many languages. Newspapers give us knowledge about many things of the past and present. Newspapers publish government policies. The statements given by the ministers, legislators and other politicians are published in the newspapers.

Newspapers publish articles, tit bits and many other things. Newspapers are useful for everybody. They publish many advertisements. They give news of the whole world. They also publish important events.

Without newspapers, people cannot get knowledge and news of our country and the world. They are an important link between the government and the people.

42. Republic Day

Republic Day is celebrated on 26th January every year. On this day in 1950, the Constitution of India was introduced. It is celebrated with great pomp and show all over the country.

Republic Day is celebrated at India Gate, New Delhi. People from all parts of the country visit this place. They watch the colourful celebrations. The procession starts at 8 a.m. and it proceeds to the Red Fort.

The procession is colourful. The Army, the Navy and the Air Force take part in this parade. The N.C.C. cadets, school boys and girls also take part in the procession. Tableaus of different states present a beautiful scene. The folk dancers gracefully stage their dances.

Air force aeroplanes leave three colourful trails in the air. This shows the three colours of our national flag. Republic Day is also celebrated in every school, college, city, town and village. It is one of the greatest national festivals of India. ●

43. The Dussehra Festival

Dussehra is an important festival of India. It is a Hindu festival. It is celebrated before Diwali. On this day, Lord Rama killed the demon king, Ravana.

People hold 'Ram Lilas' for ten days. They worship Lord Rama. During the 'Ram Lilas', there is great hustle and bustle. The effigies of Ravana, Kumbhakaran and Meghnad are built. Men women and children gather in thousands at the Ram Lila grounds.

In the evening, the tall effigies of Ravana, Kumbhakaran and Meghnad are set on fire. The crackers in the effigies burst. They are reduced to ashes.

We can learn many good things from Lord Rama's life. We can, thus, lead an ideal life. This festival teaches us the victory of good over evil. ●

44. Guru Nanak Dev

Guru Nanak Dev was the founder of the Sikh religion. He was a great saint. Guru Nanak Dev was born at Talwandi in 1469. This place is in Pakistan. It is known as Nankana Sahib.

Guru Nanak Dev spent his life in search of truth. He taught that people of all religions are the children of God. He spent his life in search of the Divine Light. He continued worshipping God.

He travelled all over the country and contacted people of different religions and sects. He said that God was one. All men are equal. He was against casteism. He was a great poet. He went to many countries of the world and preached his principles.

Guru Angad Dev was Guru Nanak's successor. We find his poetry in the Guru Granth Sahib. Guru Nanak Dev's teachings inspire millions of people all over the world. His teachings are sung in every Gurudwara by the *Granthis*. Many people benefit from his teachings. ●

45. My Favourite Book

I am fond of reading books. I have read many books. I have also read holy books such as the Ramayana, the Mahabharata and the story of Gautama, the Buddha. But the Bhagwat Gita has influenced me the most.

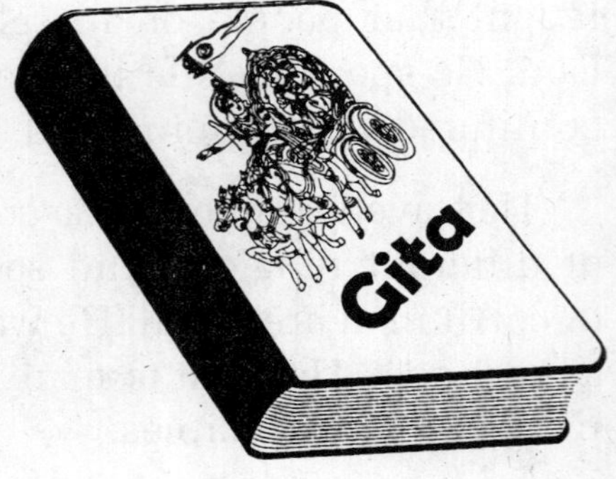

The Bhagwat Gita is a message to the human soul. Arjuna saw his own relatives and teachers in the Army of the Kauravas. So he did not want to fight a war. He requested Lord Krishna to allow him to stop fighting. Then Lord Krishna gave the sermon of the Bhagwat Gita to Arjuna.

Lord Krishna said, "Do your duty Arjuna, the human soul is immortal. It never dies. One's duty brings glory to the human soul. We should follow the course of righteousness. We should give up all evil thoughts and revert to Yogic life".

After listening to the sermon of the Bhagwat Gita, Arjuna took up arms to fight against the Kauravas.

The Bhagwat Gita contains 700 hyms. This book is not meant for any particular religion. It is written for all the human beings. It advises people to give up the evil path and follow the path of goodness.

The Bhagwat Gita has changed my life. I try to follow the path shown in this great book. ●

46. The Things I Dislike Most

Everyone has his likings and dislikings. I hate violence. It does not solve any problem. Violence is an act of the beast. It is better to use love and non-violence. Then I hate falsehood. A man tells many lies and tries to prove that he following the path of truth.

Falsehood leads to evil. I love truth and non-falsehood. I hate selfishness also. Selfishness also leads to evil. It creates hatred against other people.

I hate money-mindedness also. We should earn through our own efforts. We should not have an eye on

others' wealth. I hate arrogance also. I want to live a humble life. Pride hath a fall. It also turns man into a beast. Humility is a good habit.

I hate all these because they will make us do wrong things. We shall follow a wrong path if we have a liking for any of these. I want to lead a good life. Therefore, I want to follow the path of goodness and not evil. ●

47. An Ideal Student

An ideal student should have many qualities. He should get up early in the morning. He should go for a morning walk every day. He should take a care of his health. He should take bath everyday. He should wear clean clothes.

An ideal student should complete his home-work. He should attend the school regularly. He should show good results in the examinations. He should take part in sports and games. He should talk less and work more.

An ideal student should give respect to his teachers, parents and elders. He should love the younger students.

He should be humble and polite. He should have lovable habits. He should have good manners.

An ideal student should help the parents in household matters. He should go to bed at a fixed time. He should get up early. An ideal student should avoid smoking, drinking and other evil habits. ●

48. Things That I Love Most

I love my country most. I love Indian culture. India was worshipped as motherland by the people in olden times. India's glorious culture, the message of truth, non-violence and religious tolerance, Indian songs and dances, her sculptures, her architecture and her ancient scriptures became popular all over the world. Therefore I love India's culture.

Then I love my home. My parents take care of me at home. I live with my parents and brothers and sisters. My parents brought me up. They faced many difficulties.

I love a good moral character also. Without character, a man is like a beast. I want to speak truth, serve mankind, work hard and respect my elders. The other things which I love are birds, animals and other creations of God. ●

49. If I were the Principal of My School

If I were the Principal of my school, I would make it a very good school. I would improve the discipline of my school. Discipline is very important for every school. The classrooms would be well-furnished.

I would keep all types of books in my school if I were the Principal of my school. I would well-equip the laboratories. I would create a good atmosphere in the school. I would give more importance to co-curricular activities.

I would help develop the all-round personality of all the students. I would make physical education compulsory for all the students. I would have very friendly relations with all the teachers. I would listen to the complaints of the students. I would solve the difficulties of the teachers and students, if I were the Principal of my school. ●

50. Uses of Books

Books are our best friends. They are a great blessing. They are useful to us in many ways. When we have any problem, books give us the correct advice. They console us in our sorrows.

Books are our best companions as we never feel alone in the company of books. Books are written by very wise, experienced and intelligent persons. Therefore, they give us inspiration. Books teach us about good things and bad things. They are our best guides and philosophers.

Books fill our minds with noble thoughts. They enrich our minds. Bad books spoil our minds. Therefore, we should buy and read only good books. Our life will become very happy if we read good books. ●

51. My Daily Routine

The alarm clock wakes me up early in the morning. I want to sleep more. But I have to leave my bed. Then I go to the bathroom. I brush my teeth. I take bath, dress up and then I eat my breakfast.

In the meantime, there is the sound of the horn. It means my school bus has arrived. I pick up my school bag and rush out. I reach school at 8 a.m. I attend classes and then there is recess.

During recess I take some snacks and play for some time. Then I attend the remaining classes. I come home at 3 p.m. I take my lunch. Then I relax for some time. Then I do my school homework. My tutor comes to teach me Maths for one hour. In the evening, I play cricket in the park with my friends. Then I study for some time. I take my dinner and go for a short walk. I go to bed around 9 p.m. This is my daily routine. ●

52. Hard Work

Hard work is a great quality. All work is noble. Work is worship. Hard work is the key to success. We can progress by doing hard work. Those countries whose citizens are hard-working make great progress.

An idle person depends too much on chance. He thinks that some miracle will happen and he will become rich and prosperous. But this is not possible without hard work.

All great men of the world were very hard-working persons. By hard work, man progresses and the country progresses. Seventy years ago, Japan was a backward country. Today, Japan is one of the most prosperous countries of the world. This prosperity has been possible by means of hard work. We should all, therefore, work hard to achieve success. ●

53. Punctuality

Punctuality means to do something at the appointed time. One who is punctual is liked by all. He can achieve success in life. Time is the most valuable possession of man.

Unfortunately, very few people are punctual in our country. They waste the time of others. They waste their own time too. Many students reach the class late. They disturb the teacher and the other students of their class. Many people are in the habit of reaching their office late. The work of the public suffers. Their own work also suffers.

In India, people are very careless about punctuality. But in the Western countries, people know the value of being on time. We should be punctual in everything. By doing so, we can do our work properly and can help the society to work smoothly. ●

54. Value of Trees

Trees are very useful to man. They support the life of living beings. The green leaves of trees absorb carbon dioxide and break it up into carbon and oxygen.

Thus trees replace oxygen which is constantly used up and changed into carbon dioxide in breathing and burning. The trees retain carbon and release oxygen for the use of living beings.

Trees help to prevent drought and floods. Man has not recognised the importance of trees. Man cuts down trees to get quick profit from them. We should plant more and more trees. We should not cut them down. Man can live a happy life only if he plants more trees. We can inhale fresh air if we have more trees on this earth. ●

55. Social Service and Students

Man is a social animal. He cannot live alone. Society takes care of all the persons. It provides us comforts and other facilities. Therefore, it is the duty of everybody to do service to the society.

Students have much strength and energy. They have no worries about earning their bread. So, they should provide help in the field of social service. Eighty per cent of our population lives in villages. Many villagers are illiterate. They do not know about their rights and duties. Students can put in their best efforts to improve the condition of the villagers.

Students can go to the villages during vacation and provide help to the villagers. They can also help other non-governmental social organisations. Thus, students can put their energy to the best use by doing some kind of social service. ●

56. Holidays

Holidays provide a great change to students. They have a great significance for students. During the holidays, students are free from the burden of books. Students can devote time to their favourite pursuits.

Holidays are fun. These are the days of feasting and merry-making. Some teachers burden the students with holiday homework. This is not good. Students can be encouraged to do some kind of social work during holidays.

All work and no holiday makes a student's life dull and boring. For some students, holidays mean more work. They overburden themselves with work. This is not a good idea of spending holidays. A holiday is a free time and it should be spent in this spirit only. A holiday can bring great joy, if it is spent as a holiday. ●

57. Health is Wealth

There is no doubt that health is wealth. If a wealthy person is not healthy, he cannot enjoy life. On the other hand, a poor man with good health can really enjoy his life.

A rich man without good health can not enjoy good sleep. He cannot eat proper food. He has to live with precautions and preventions. On the other hand, a poor but healthy man enjoys life better. He works hard and enjoys sound sleep. He suffers from no disease. He does not spend sleepless and restless nights.

Therefore, it is better to have good health. We can enjoy food, work hard have sound sleep and can find happiness in our life. Thus, a poor but healthy man is better than a rich but sick man. ●

58. Educational Value of Travelling

All modern means of transport have made travelling very easy. Today, we have buses, cars, railways, aeroplanes, ships and many other means of travelling.

Travelling has great educative value. It teaches better than books. Bookish knowledge is theoretical. Travelling makes us see things, people and places with our own eyes.

Subjects like history, geography and social sciences can be better learnt through travelling. We come in contact

with other people by travelling. We come to know about their habits, customs and traditions. Thus our outlook is widened.

Educational tours arranged by schools promote inter-state and international goodwill. They strengthen the relations of friendship among various states and countries.

59. An Ideal Citizen

An ideal citizen knows his rights and responsibilities. He thinks of the nation first and of himself later. He respects the rights of others. He serves his country and his fellow-men.

He does not claim any special favour for himself. He respects the laws of the country. He has great civic sense. He does not waste water and electricity. He does not misuse the facilities provided to him.

An ideal citizen does not cheat the government. He does not indulge in anti-social activities. He is against smuggling, corruption, hoarding and black-marketing.

An ideal citizen is a thorough gentleman. He is polite and courteous. He is cooperative and considerate. He does not hurt the feelings of others. An ideal citizen is a valuable asset to the society. ●

60. Value of Discipline

Discipline is very important in a civilised life. Discipline can be defined as control over one's desires and obedience to codes of behaviour. If there is no discipline, there will be confusion everywhere.

Discipline is of great importance in schools. If there is no discipline in schools, it is not possible to impart education effectively. It is necessary to maintain law and order in the society.

There should be discipline at home also. Children must be taught self-control. Parents themselves should keep discipline. Children should be taught the value of discipline in childhood. A country can not face external wars if its armed forces are not disciplined.

Unfortunately, there is not much discipline today in schools, colleges and government offices. That is why India is facing many problems.

Discipline is necessary for people in all walks of life. Students studying in schools and colleges, Defence personnel, industrial workers — all must have discipline. Only then a nation can progress. ●

61. Growing Population or Family Planning or Population Explosion

The population of India has increased at an alarming rate after Independence. Because of over-population, there is poverty. The increase in population is due to the fall in death rate. There is better medical facility and the death rate has, therefore fallen.

Because of over-population, there is unemployment, poverty and food problem. There are many reasons of over-population. The poor people have more children. They think that children are the gifts of God. Some people think that a man who has many sons and daughters is a lucky person. Parents who have only daughters go on producing children until they have a son.

It is necessary to solve the problem of over-population. Family planning should be adopted to control the birth of children. Uneducated people should be made aware through various programmes that having more children is a burden on them and the couples who have one or two children should be given awards. ●

62. A Street Hawker

We see street hawkers every day. Street hawkers are found in every city. A street hawker carries his things on his head. Some street hawkers carry their wares on a cycle or a hand-cart.

A street hawker sells things like vegetables, fruit, ice-cream, candies, eatables, sweets and various things of

daily use. He goes from one street to another to sell his wares. He shouts in the street in an interesting tone. Some street hawkers ring bells, some make strange sounds and some sing songs to attract the attention of the customers.

The customers of a street hawker are generally housewives and children. The housewives buy vegetables and fruit from him. The children buy ice-cream, toys, sweets and candies.

A street hawker has no fixed price. People bargain with him before buying things. Some street hawkers are not clean. They do not cover their eatables from dust and flies. We should not buy eatables from such street hawkers. ●

63. A Street Beggar

Street beggars are seen everywhere in our country. We find them begging at railway stations, bus stops, temples, in streets, bazaars and at traffic-signals.

Some street beggars are very clever. They make the hearts of the people melt. People take pity on them and give them something. They wear dirty and shabby clothes. They want money, clothes, grain, food or anything else. Some beggars beg in the name of God.

Some street beggars are thieves who cheat people and steal their things. Some beggars are disabled. We should give alms only to the disabled beggars. We should not give anything to those beggars who are healthy but pose to be disabled. Healthy beggars can do work but they don't want to. They get easy money by begging. Sometimes they get more than the persons who earn their living by doing hard work for long hours.

Begging brings a bad name to the society and country. If a healthy person is found begging, he should be punished by the law. ●

64. Pt. Jawahar Lal Nehru

Pt. Jawahar Lal Nehru was the first Prime Minister of India. He was a very popular national leader. He was respected by people of all castes and creeds. He was born on 14th November 1889 at Allahabad. He belonged to a wealthy Brahmin family. His father, Pt. Moti Lal Nehru was a great lawyer.

Pt. Jawahar Lal Nehru received his education at Harrow School and Trinity College, Cambridge and returned to India. He became a follower of Mahatma Gandhi. He toured the country and joined the struggle for freedom started by Mahatma Gandhi. He became the President of the Indian National Congress. He wanted to achieve complete freedom for the country. India became free on 15th August 1947.

Nehru was a great leader. He tried to solve the difficult problems of our country. India became strong during his primeministership. He worked for the uplift of the country. He loved peace and did his best to bring peace to the world. Nehru died on 26th May, 1964. He is still remembered as "Chacha Nehru".

65. My Motherland

India is my mother country. I love my motherland very much. India is a very big country. From the Himalayas down to Kanyakumari, India spreads out over a vast area. She spreads out from the Assam Hills in the east to the Bay of Kutch in the west.

India's population is about a hundred crores. Most of India's population lives in villages. Agriculture is the main source of income of the villagers.

India has a rich culture. She is an ancient land. She possesses rich traditions. India has shown the path of light to other countries. India is proud of her ancient literature — the Vedas, the Upanishads, the Bhagwat Gita and the Puranas.

India was known as the 'Golden Sparrow' as she possessed rich natural resources. India has a vast system of rivers and canals. We produce wheat, rice, oil seeds, cotton and spices. India has beautiful mountain ranges, deep forests, flora and fauna and the rich fields. India got freedom in 1947 after a great freedom struggle. India is now a glorious land.

66. A Pleasant Dream

I had a pleasant dream last night. I went to bed late and was fast asleep. Suddenly I felt that I was in the fairyland. There was a big garden. Flowers were blooming. The fairies were singing beautiful songs.

One fairy came to me and greeted me with a sweet smile. She offered me a small chair to sit on and enjoy the dance. Then I saw a little child playing on the flute. He arrived in the midst of the fairies. The child started dancing with the fairies. There were some dwarfs sitting

nearby. There was a beautiful river. The sun was shining and a cool breeze was blowing.

I sat under a shady tree. The tree was laden with fruit. The child brought some fruit for me. Then the child started singing and dancing. The fairies stood around me. It was a beautiful scene.

When I was taking fruit and enjoying dancing, I suddenly woke up. My mother asked me to get up and prepare for school. ●

67. A Rainy Day in Summer

There is great heat in summer in India. The rainy days that follow are a blessing. The rain is useful for crops and trees. The weather becomes pleasant and cool on a rainy day.

One day, in summer, the clouds appeared in the sky. It started to drizzle. Soon the drizzle changed into a heavy rain. The drains started overflowing with water. The streets turned into small streams.

The children were very happy. They made paper boats and started floating them. It became very pleasant and cool. There was great joy. But there was mud everywhere. The ground became slippery. Some old buildings collapsed. Many trees got uprooted.

Although there was a lot of inconvenience, yet the people were very happy. The joy of the people ended soon. The rain stopped, the sun came out and the weather became very hot again. ●

68. An Indian Juggler

We find jugglers in different streets of a town or a village. The people enjoy their tricks. A juggler carries a bag on his shoulder. A young chap follows him. He may be his son.

A juggler carries his things and places them in a corner of a street. He earns his bread with this stock of articles. The sound of the drums attracts children and they rush out to watch the juggler's show. The clever tricks of the juggler entertain the people very much.

A juggler starts his show with playing-card tricks and sometimes he starts his show with a little monkey. He holds a rupee coin and spins it into the air. Then he takes out his magic wand and closes his fist, with the rupee coin in and it becomes a five-rupee note. People cheer him. With a little basket, he moves around and collects small coins. The children give him money. He entertains children and other people. His feats of skill are enjoyed much by the people.

69. A Drowning Tragedy

I had a holiday last week. So I along with some of my friends went to the Okhla lake. We hired a boat and started rowing. We ate apples and sweets. We all sang songs of joy.

Suddenly, we heard a cry of alarm. We soon rushed to the spot in our boat. We saw that a man was getting drowned in the lake. He was crying for help.

This man was not a good swimmer but he had decided to swim. The water current was swift. He could not swim across the lake. We shouted at the top of our voices.

Some people on the other side of the river heard our voices and they jumped into the river.

They were able to catch the man. He was pulled into our boat. We reached the bank. The water was taken out of the man's belly. Artificial respiration was also given. Fortunately, a tragedy was averted. The man was saved.

70. A Flight in an Aeroplane or An Enjoyable Travelling Experience

My father had some urgent business at Jaipur. He wanted to reach there soon. So he decided to go by an aeroplane. He wanted to take me along. We packed a small bag and went to the airport.

There were a number of aeroplanes at the airport. Many people had come to see off their relatives and friends. We entered the aeroplane. This was my first experience of travelling by air.

The aeroplane took off into the air. It flew higher and higher. I felt a little giddy. I looked out through the window. Everything looked very small. Very big trees looked very small. Huge buildings looked like small huts. The big river looked like a snake.

Now Jaipur was in sight. The aeroplane started flying down. It landed at Jaipur airport. We thanked God that we had landed safely. It was one of the most memorable journeys I ever had in my life. ●

71. A Marriage Procession

A marriage procession is a good show of rejoicing. The bridegroom sits on a white mare. He wears saffron and silken clothes and wreaths of flowers. They hang from his head and cover his face. His hands are dyed red with henna. A beautiful paper canopy is placed on his head. He is the hero of the marriage procession.

There are batches of women wearing fine clothes. Males and children also follow this procession. The band plays on beautiful tunes. The atmosphere is bright and gay.

Gas lamps are carried by a few persons. Crackers are burst. There is a beautiful display of fire-works. Relatives and friends of the bridegroom sing and dance.

When the marriage procession reaches the bride's house, they are welcomed by one and all, They are served with cold and hot drinks. After that they enjoy a rich feast. After taking food, people leave for their homes. The bride and bridegroom perform marriage rites. ●

72. An Indian Coolie

Coolies are found at the railway stations, bus stands and tonga stands. They carry luggage on their heads.

A coolie is always available to give his service. He leads a humble and honest life. He is healthy and strong. Some coolies can carry very heavy loads.

A coolie lives on the wages he earns. He does not work under any firm. He leads an independent life. He is free to work or rest. Earning a livelihood is a difficult job for him.

A coolie does not lead an easy life. He has to support his family. Therefore he has to earn enough money. A coolie has to work in the very busy areas of the cities or towns. A coolie is a labourer. It is our duty to pay him reasonable labour as he belongs to the poor section of the society. ●

73. The Post Office

Post offices are located in every town, village and city. In a big town or city, there are many post offices and their branches. But in a small village, there is one post office only.

It is a very useful department for the public. Post offices carry our messages to distant places. The charges are not very high. We may keep in touch with our friends and relatives through post offices.

We put our letters in the letter boxes and our letters reach our friends and relatives. There are a number of windows in the post office. We can send registered letters, parcels and money-orders. We can also get post cards, inland letters and envelopes at these windows.

The Post office also distributes mail. The postmen deliver the letters in the homes of the addressees or at business places.

The staff of the post office works day in and day out. We must admire their hard work. Post offices are very useful to the citizens. Without a post office, life would become dull. ●

74. My Favourite Game

Hockey is my favourite game. Hockey is played with eleven players on each side. There is one goal-keeper, two fullbacks, three half backs and five forwards. Hockey is played on grassy fields.

The game starts with a bully-off at the centre between the centre forwards of the rival teams. Players carry off the ball and then try to pass it through the goal posts of the opposite teams. They hit the ball hard from their side to the side of the rivals. Whichever team scores more goals, wins the match.

There are two referees who conduct the match. If there is foul play, they penalise it. If the ball crosses the boundary line, the game is started again.

I love to play hockey. It provides excellent exercise to all parts of the body. This game develops team spirit. It amuses and excites. The players feel a sensation of joy. My heart is filled with joy when I play or watch a hockey match.

75. The Coldest Day in Winter

Winter is the coldest season in the year. This year 15th January was the coldest day of the season. The temperature fell below freezing point. It was a frosty day. The cold winds bit and burnt our faces. Water had an icy touch. Our teeth started chattering. The fingers refused to work.

Every one liked to stay indoors. In the morning and evening, frost spread everywhere in the atmosphere. We sat beside the glowing hearth. Some people used electric heaters.

Cold and biting winds blew and people remained within their rooms. Sometimes, it rained. We had to save ourselves from cold. Everyone used woollen clothes. The women wore warm shawls. People closed their business before time during the coldest evening. Every one took extra precaution to save himself from pneumonia. The weak and the old cursed the coldest day of the season.

76. A Policeman

A policeman is a familiar figure. He is found everywhere in his uniform. He performs his duty in the city streets, railway platforms, inter-state bus stands and at other places. He carries a stick and whistle in his hand.

He is a useful servant. He maintains order and peace. He wants us to obey the law of the land. Maintenance of law is his duty. It is his duty to protect the life and property of the people. He is a terror to the bad characters.

A policeman performs very hard duty. Many people do not like a policeman because he is rough. People do not like policemen because they think that all policemen are corrupt and dishonest. But some policemen are very honest and polite.

In big cities where the law and order situation goes bad, it is the policeman who comes to the rescue of the people. The policeman uses force if there is danger to the lives of citizens. The policeman should be honest, polite, kind and literate to serve the people. It is our duty to cooperate with him. ●

77. A Day in the Life of a Teacher

A teacher works to build our nation. The profession of a teacher is not easy. He works hard like a student. He solves the difficulties of all the students regarding their lessons.

A teacher gets up early in the morning. He prepares his lessons. He plans his lessons with great care. He reaches his school in time. He remains busy the whole day. He teaches many classes. All through the day, he works with his students. He had to attend many periods. He works till evening. He returns home very tired.

He takes a little rest and starts work again. He has to evaluate the answer sheets of the students. Sometimes he brings the note-books of the students to his home. He evaluates the answers of the note-books. At night, the teacher reads his books and prepares new lessons. He sleeps for a few hours. He wakes up again early in the morning and gets ready for the school. It is his daily routine.

We respect the teachers because they make us what we want to become in life. ●

78. Hostel Life

Hostel life has many advantages. A large number of students come from villages, towns and cities and they stay in a hostel. Students stay in hostels and they study also.

The students in the hostels are looked after by the warden. They do not have any worry. The senior students provide help to the junior students in the hostel. Mutual cooperation in studies and sports and games raises the standard of a boarder.

Students develop the qualities of self-help in a hostel. They do not get any help here from their parents or brothers and sisters. They have to depend upon themselves. They live by themselves. Arrangement of their food is made by the warden. The students have to pay for the food and stay in the hostel.

Both the rich and poor students live in hostels. The atmosphere is more disciplined in a hostel than it is at home. Students achieve their goal of education and discipline in a hostel. One should not waste one's time and one should not mix up with the bad boys in a hostel. Hostel life has its own charm. ●

79. Autobiography of a Rupee

I am a coin. I am called 'a rupee' by everyone. Everyone wants to own me. I am made of a metal. The metal has to pass through many stages in the furnaces of a mint. On one side of me is written 'one rupee' and on the other side, there is the emblem of the country.

I cannot be destroyed easily. I play the role of a helper.

When salary is given to the employees, I am needed badly. I am required in every shop.

People are respected in the society if they have me in plenty. Hard labour is required to own me. No one can satisfy his wants without me. In the form of a metal, I am a coin. In the form of a currency note, I am made of paper printed on both sides. A coin of a metal and a currency note have the same value.

I am a friend of the poor people. They have to work very hard to own me. ●

80. Independence Day

Before 15th August, 1947, India was ruled by the Britishers. India became free on 15th August 1947. This day is celebrated as Independence Day every year.

On this day in 1947, our first Prime Minster Jawahar Lal Nehru, hoisted the National Flag at the Red Fort in Delhi. He also delivered a message to the nation. Since then it is celebrated every year at the Red Fort. A large number of men, women and children come to watch the celebrations.

A salute of twenty one guns is fired and the National Anthem is played. The Prime Minister delivers a message to the nation. This day is celebrated in every part of India.

In the schools, the Principals hoist the National Flag and deliver speeches. At night the national buildings are illuminated. Many people celebrate this day by flying kites. The day reminds us of the sacrifice made by the patriots and martyrs. ●

SECTION 3

PARAGRAPHS

1. Hard Work

Hard work is the most valuable possession of man. An idler depends on chance. He sits with folded hands. He waits for some golden chance that will come his way. He keeps on sitting while others keep on working hard. They are able to achieve what they want. Hard work alone can make us successful and happy. All great men of the world did hard work. They never bothered about the nature of work. All work is noble. In fact, work is worship. If the citizens of a country are hard working, the country will certainly progress. Japan was a backward country a few years ago. But today it is one of the most prosperous countries in the world. All this is possible by means of hard work. ●

2. Punctuality

Punctuality is a necessary habit in all public affairs. Nothing can be brought to a conclusion without punctuality. Time is the most valuable possession of man in a civilised society. Punctuality means doing something at the fixed or appointed time. But very few people are punctual. People who are not punctual waste the time of others and their own time also. Many students are in the habit of reaching school late. Thus, they disturb the class. Many people reach their offices late. The public suffers and their own work also suffers. In India, people are very careless about punctuality. In the Western countries, people know the value of punctuality. Once Churchill's secretary reached office late by five minutes. When he was asked the reason for his late coming, the secretary said, "My watch is, perhaps, slow". At this, Churchill remarked "Either you change your watch or I shall have to change my secretary". ●

3. Childhood Days

The best years of one's life are the childhood days. The sweet memories of this period are glorious. They have the freshness of a dream. A child has no responsibilities. He is looked after by his parents. He gets everything without doing anything. A child enjoys perfect freedom. He has no worries, no hardships and no troubles. He can say anything to anybody. If a child does something wrong, he is generally excused. Even his meaningless chatter is a source of joy. A child's life is full of innocence. He builds castles of sand and feels very happy. He gets joy in floating paperboats. He often quarrels with others over small things but soon forgets about it. Childhood is really the golden period of one's life. ●

4. A Rainy Day in Winter

A rainy day in winter is unwelcome. 23rd January was one of such days. The whole city of Delhi was in the grip of a terrible cold wave. Dark and thick clouds were thundering in the sky. In the early hours of morning, a heavy downpour started. There was a hail storm also. The storm continued for one hour. Roads were blocked. Traffic came to a standstill. The weather became very bad. No one wanted to go out of his house. The city presented a deserted look. Very few people could be seen moving on the roads. The government employees took casual leave. The attendance in schools and colleges was very thin. The rain and hail storm caused heavy damage. Many trees were uprooted. Telephone wires broke and many telephones became dead. The poor people suffered a lot. The cold increased terribly and bone-chilling winds started blowing. ●

5. An Honest Person I have Known

Honesty is the best policy. It is an old saying. In fact, all people should be honest. But it is very rare to find an honest person these days. However, I have known a person who impressed me deeply with his honesty. One day I was travelling in a D.T.C. bus. I lost my brief-case. The brief-case contained some important documents and one thousand rupees. I was much worried. After some time a man came to my house. He was shabbily dressed. He was a stranger. He gave me my brief-case. The documents and money was intact in it. He told me that he had found it in the D.T.C. bus. He had found my identity card in the brief-case and came to know my name and address. I was very impressed by his honesty. He refused to accept the reward which I tried to give him. He was just a poor rickshaw-puller. ●

6. The Neighbour I Dislike

A bad neighbour makes hell of our life. I have one such neighbour. His name is Ram Lal. He runs a small shop. He has four sons and three daughters. Their house is like a fish market. The sons and the daughters are always quarrelling among themselves. Their mother keeps on shouting with them. The children are always ready to pick up a quarrel with anyone. The eldest son is a spoilt child. He has failed in the eighth class three times. He cares less for his books and more for his clothes and hairstyle. He teases the young boys and girls of the locality. All the neighbours are fed up with this family. ●

7. An Ideal Teacher

An ideal teacher knows the art of teaching. He is the master of his subject. He makes his lessons interesting. His method of teaching is convincing and inspiring. An ideal teacher treats his students like his own children. He praises the good work done by them. If a student does some mistake, he is not very harsh to him. He tactfully makes his student realise his mistake. An ideal teacher is never angry with his students. He believes in simple living and high thinking. He never sets a wrong example before his students. He has a high moral character. An ideal teacher himself practises whatever he preaches to his students. He is a true friend and a sincere guide to the students. ●

8. The Clown in a Circus Show

The clown in a circus show plays an important role. He entertains the people. He makes funny gestures and remarks. His appearance too is very funny. He paints his face and puts on a multi-coloured dress. He also puts on a strange-looking cap. The spectators begin to laugh as soon as the clown enters the ring. They enjoy the clown's antics and his remarks about the other actors. He looks a foolish clown but actually he is a skilled artiste. He can imitate actions of the other actors successfully. People get a pleasant surprise when the clown starts dancing on the rope or wire. He also rides the galloping horses. The clown appears during the interval between one feat and the other and makes the spectators laugh heartily. ●

9. My Grandmother

My grandmother is an old lady. She reads holy books. She may miss her meals but she does not miss going to the temple. She has a wrinkled face and silvery hair. She is fat, short and slightly bent. She keeps one hand on her waist and she rolls the beads of the rosary with the other hand. She is God-fearing. Her lips are always moving in silent prayer. She is a very religious lady. She feeds sparrows and dogs with chapatis. My grandmother is fond of me. ●

10. The Season I Like Most

I like spring season most. During this season it is neither too cold nor too hot. In spring season, the nights are cold but the days are sunny. Spring season is the best time for doing any work. Also, it is the best time to study and play. During spring season, Nature is at its best. Flowers bloom and trees put out new leaves. There is a new look everywhere on the earth. Spring season has a healthy effect on the body. New blood is formed. There is hardly any disease. During spring season, we can work for more time. We feel healthy and happy. Our capacity to work increases. It is the season of flowers and fruits. It is also the season of colour and beauty. Everyone looks fresh and is full of energy. It is the season of picnics and outings. ●

11. The Things I Do Not Like

Every man has his own likes and dislikes. I do not like showy and multi-coloured clothes. They give a look of cheapness. I do not like summer season also. In the blazing sun I cannot go out. I remain confined to my room. I do not like appearing in examinations as they suck my blood. I do not like serious-natured people. I do not like the sermons of old people. I hate cheats and fair-weather friends. Above all, I hate all those persons who indulge in anti-social and anti-national activities. ●

12. Uses of Books

Books are a great blessing. They are useful to us in many ways. They are our best friends. When we are in trouble, books stand by us and give us the right advice. Books console us in our sorrows. We never feel alone in the company of books. Books are written by experienced persons who are wise and who have matured minds. They are, therefore, our best guides and philosophers, when we are in some confusion. Books give us inspiration to do great things. They fill our minds with noble thoughts. They improve our minds and awaken our souls. But bad books poison our minds. We should therefore select and read good books only. ●

13. An Exhibition You Have Seen

Last Sunday I went to see an exhibition. It was organised by the Department of Small-Scale Industries. It was at Pragati Maidan. There were large crowds of people in the exhibition. They were in their best dresses. It looked like a big fair. Almost all the States had set up their pavilions. The articles made in small scale industries were displayed in the exhibition. There were electrical appliances, hosiery and readymade garments, sport goods, plastic toys etc. There was a great rush at the stalls selling eatables. Merry-go-rounds were a great attraction for the children. I had a very happy time in the exhibition. This visit was very rewarding. ●

14. If I were the Principal of Our School

If I were the Principal of my school, I would do my best to make my school an ideal institution. I will give attention to discipline. A school cannot function smoothly without discipline. If I were the Principal of my school I would ensure that the laboratories were well equipped. The library would have books of all kinds. All this would help to create a good atmosphere in the school. I would give due place to co-curricular activities. I would make efforts to develop all round personality of the students. Physical education would be compulsory for all students. I would hear the complaints of all the students. I would have friendly relations with the members of my staff. I would get the cooperation of all my staff members. I would improve the academic performance of all the students. ●

15. Waiting for the Postman

We are living in an age of hurry and worry. Day and night, we are busy earning our livelihood. We are miles away from our friends and relatives. We have no time to visit them. But we always want to know about their welfare. So we wait for the postman eagerly. Sometimes, we wait for him impatiently. The postman brings us news from our friends and relatives. He may sometimes bring sad news but we still wait for him. Whenever there is a knock at the door, we rush to open the door. We want to see whether the person knocking is the postman. When our friend or relative is sick we wait for the postman. We want to know the welfare of the person. Everyone of us waits for the postman whether he brings something for us or not. ●

16. The Recess Period or Lunch Break at School

As soon as the recess bell goes, students rush out of their classrooms. Some students go to the school canteen. They spend their pocket money and relish sweet dishes. The school play ground also becomes alive with the students. The players take part in different games. They get back their energy and feel relaxed. There is a great rush in the school library. Some students get books issued and others return books. All the students make the best use of this period. They relax and entertain themselves in their own way. For sometime, they forget about studies. When the recess period is over, they get back to their classrooms to start their studies again. ●

17. A Scene at a Railway Station

The railway station presents an interesting scene. There is a great rush at the booking windows. There is also a great rush of passengers at the inquiry office. The coolies are seen sitting in a row. As soon as a train arrives, they rush towards it. Vendors shout their wares at the top of their voices. When a train arrives, there is a lot of noise and confusion. There is a great rush at the doors of the compartments. Every one wants to get in first. Many passengers get down from the train and many get in.

After some time, the guard blows the whistle and waves the green flag. The train moves and leaves the platform. Those who have come to receive or see off their relatives leave for home. Soon the platform wears a deserted look. ●

18. My Hobby

Different people have different hobbies. A hobby is taken up in spare time. It gives us joy in our spare time. My hobby is gardening. I took to this hobby when I went to see my uncle at his village. The green crops, tall trees and beautiful flowers left a deep impression on me. After coming back from my uncle's home, I developed the backyard of my house. I made it into a beautiful garden. It has flower plants and fruit trees. There are fifty varieties of roses in my garden. My garden is very dear to me. I spend two hours daily in my garden. It gives me a great pleasure. It also gives me exercise. My friends and guests praise my garden. I don't allow anyone to pluck flowers from my garden. My hobby has changed my life. ●

19. Look Before You Leap

We should think carefully before we do something. We should take precaution and do deep thinking. Then only we should decide to do something. Some people are impulsive by nature. They do not think before doing a thing. They act rashly and then repent. We should do thorough calculation and also we should do thorough survey. We should invest money in business only if we have experience in business. If we do not have knowledge we can take guidance from experienced persons in business. We should make a thorough study before starting a business. Similarly, if we want to swim across a river, we should first see whether we can cross or not. We should not start swimming without thinking about our experience and depth of the river. If we take action rashly or foolishly, it may ruin us. ●

20. Slow and Steady Wins the Race

It is rightly said that slow and steady wins the race. It means that regular work pays in the end. Therefore, we should work in a methodical manner. Regularity, punctuality and steadfastness bring success. A man who does his work slowly and steadily will not make many mistakes. He remains alert about the mistakes. His work will be superior in quality. Those who do their work in haste commit many mistakes. Haste makes waste. Therefore, we should not do anything in haste. Only regular and punctual work brings success in life. ●

21. Try, Try Again

When we do something, we expect success. If we do not get success, we become sad and depressed. We stop trying again. It is wrong on our part. We should not expect that we must always succeed. If we fail, we should try to know the reason of our failure. Each failure teaches us something. It has been rightly said : "Failure is the stepping stone to success". We should calmly try to find out the reason of our failure. Then we should try again. Even if we fail for the second time, we should not give up effort. We should try again. Constant effort brings success at last. We should keep on trying, trying and trying again. ●

22. Silence is Gold

Speech is a great blessing of God. Everyone has the gift of speech. But it is rightly said that silence is gold. If each one of us begins to speak at the same time, nothing will be understandable. Therefore, we should know when we should remain silent. Silence is the quality of a good speaker. It is a great quality to be a good listener. A man who speaks too much is not liked much. Such a man exposes himself. If a man remains silent, he is considered a deep man. Our silence hides most of our weaknesses and shortcomings. It gives us an opportunity to listen to others. We can benefit from others' talk and experience. Therefore it is said, "If speech is silver, silence is gold".

●

23. All that Glitters is not Gold

Gold is a bright and shining metal. There are other metals which are equally shining and bright. But they have no quality. Similarly, there are many things in the world which are not what they seem. This is true of human beings also. There are many persons who seem to be good persons but they do many evil things. So, we cannot judge a man from his appearance. An innocent looking man may be a cheat. A man with a smile on his face may do some harm to us. A man who says that he is our best friend, may stab us in the back. We should not be misled by the outward show. ●

24. Examinations

Examinations are a horror to students. They are a necessary evil. Many students do not like examinations. They give tension. Every student has fear of the examination. Examination is like a fever. If a student feels nervous, he cannot learn anything. He spends sleepless nights. Examinations are not the sure test of students' ability. Examination is test of cramming, not of knowledge. It is not possible to test in three hours what a student has learnt during the whole year. It is a matter of chance if a student gets the same questions which he has learnt by heart. Those students who do not study the whole year, try to copy in the examination. There are both advantages and disadvantages in examination system. But we can not remove examinations. ●

25. Health is Wealth

There is no doubt that health is wealth. A wealthy man with poor health cannot enjoy his life. All his wealth is useless for him. Money can not buy health and happiness. On the other hand, a poor man with good health can enjoy life. A rich man with poor health cannot enjoy a sound sleep. He cannot enjoy good food. He spends his life under many precautions and preventions. On the other hand, a poor but healthy man lives a better life. He can work hard and enjoys a sound sleep. He does not spend sleepless and restless nights. He can eat what ever he wishes. Thus, a poor but healthy man can live a better life than a rich but sick man. ●

26. A Summer Day without Electricity

Electricity has become a very important part of our life. We are much dependent on electricity. If there is no electricity, life seems to stop. We feel restless without electricity. On a hot summer day, when there is no electricity, we start pacing up and down. There seems to be no life without electricity. We sweat a lot. We can not work. We can not study and we can not concentrate in any thing if there is no electricity. We call up the electricity office again and again. We want that electricity should be restored immediately. We pass the time under great stress. When the electricity is restored, we heave a sigh of relief. ●

27. A Scene at a Milk Booth

In big cities such as Delhi, milk is sold at milk booths. At these booths, there is always a queue for buying milk in the morning and in the evening. People stand in a queue and one by one they move on to the window. Each person pays the money for the milk according to requirement. He gets special counters. Then he moves on to the machine with a slot to insert the counter. Only one counter can be inserted at a time into the slot. Then half a litre of milk is poured into the vessel. People are in a hurry to get to the window or the machine. Sometimes, some people try to break the queue. This leads to small arguments and quarrels. Some wise persons in the queue are able to stop these quarrels. ●

28. The Rainbow

Rainbow appears in the sky at the end of the rain. It is a long and wide band of seven colours. It forms a semi-circle going from one end of the earth to the other. Scientists say that when sunlight passes through a thin medium to a denser medium, all the seven colours which are present in the white light, form a semi-circular rainbow. The seven colours are violet, indigo, blue, green, yellow, orange and red. People believe that if a rainbow appears after the rain, it is an indication that there will be no more rains. In Hindi, rainbow is called *'Indra Dhanush'* which means the Bow of Lord Indra. According to Hindu mythology Lord Indra is the god of rain. The rainbow looks miraculously beautiful. Its sight is very soothing to the eye. Small children get very excited when they see a rainbow. ●

29. The Rain

Rain comes as a welcome relief after the heat and dust of the summer. Rain is a wonderful gift of Nature to all mankind. If there are no rains, crops will not grow. All the vegetation will wither away. We cannot think of life on this planet without rain. Without rains, the water level of the earth will sink. The people will not get water to drink and food to eat. There will be a terrible drought. Water is life and without rain there will be no life on the earth. People wait for rain eagerly, when they are delayed. We should thank God for this great gift He has given to all mankind. ●

30. A Holiday

I had a holiday from school last week. I, along with my friends, went to the lake to enjoy ourselves. We took our fishing rods and kites with us. We went on foot and were a little tired on reaching the lake. We rested for some time. Then we flew kites. As it was a windy day, kite flying was a joyful experience. Then we enjoyed fishing in the lake. Now we were hungry. We unpacked our baskets and ate sweets, fruits and some snacks. It was getting dark. We enjoyed the beautiful sight of the setting sun. We returned to our homes. It was a wonderful outing on a holiday. ●

31. My Favourite Festival — Diwali

Diwali is my favourite festival. It is the festival of lights. It is celebrated in all parts of our country. A few days before Diwali, people clean their houses and shops and get them whitewashed. On Diwali day, people decorate their houses. On the night of Diwali, lamps are lit in every village, town and city. All the houses, shops and buildings are illuminated with earthern lamps, candles and electric bulbs. Children move about in their best clothes. People exchange sweets and gifts. Children spend money in buying sweets, toys and crackers. At night people worship 'Laxmi', the goddess of wealth. Diwali is a festival of joy. On this day every one is happy and gay. ●

32. A Day without Water

Water is the greatest gift of God to mankind. When water supply is normal, we don't care about the importance of water. We use it carelessly. Rather, we waste a lot of water.But when the taps are dry, we become very worried. All work comes to a standstill. When there is no water we cannot do washing, cleaning or bathing. We cannot cook our meals and have no water to drink. People run to all places in search of water, carrying cans and buckets. The day without water causes a lot of problems and hardships. A day without water only makes us realise the importance of water. ●

33. The Postman

A postman puts on a uniform. He brings our letters, money-orders, parcels and registered letters. Everyone waits for the postman eagerly. The work of the postman is not easy. He has to work hard throughout the day. He goes to the post office every morning. He sorts the letters there. Then he goes to his area to deliver letters. All the people of his area know the postman very well. He is a government servant. He does not get a very good pay. He gets a poor salary and leads a hard life. ●

34. The Farmer

The Indian farmer is a simple villager. He leads a humble life. Most of the farmers can neither read nor write. The life of a farmer is hard. He works in his fields in all weathers. He gets up before dawn. He goes to his fields and works there the whole day. He returns home at sun set. He ploughs the fields and then he sows the seeds. And finally he harvests the crops. Farmer grows different kinds of crops. He gives us wheat and maize for our bread and gives sugar for our tea. He gives us cotton for clothes. He lives a simple, healthy and useful life. A farmer does a great service to all of us. Without a farmer, we will all starve. ●

35. A Morning Walk

A morning walk is a very useful exercise. It is a light exercise. It refreshes our body and mind. In the morning, Nature is at its best. A morning walk brings us in contact with the beautiful surroundings of Nature. It gives us a great joy and also keeps us fit and healthy. The green grass, the blossoming flowers, chirping birds, the fresh air, the rising sun and morning dew — all provide us great joy and they fill our heart with happiness. Morning walk is good for all. The old and the young, the healthy and the weak, all should take a morning walk. ●

36. Value of Trees

Trees are very useful to man. They support the life of living things. Trees are needed for making paper, furniture and houses. They are used in every thing. When we breathe and burn, we produce carbon dioxide. Trees replace this carbon dioxide with oxygen. The green leaves of trees absorb carbon dioxide and break it up into carbon and oxygen. The leaves keep carbon and release oxygen for the use of living beings. Trees prevent drought and floods. Man has cut down trees in large numbers and he is cutting more and more trees. Man must stop cutting more trees, otherwise he will suffer greatly. ●

37. Holi

Many festivals are celebrated in India. Holi is one of them. Holi is an important festival of the Hindus. It is a festival of colours and fun. A night before Holi, a big fire is burnt. Holi has a religious background. King Hiranyakashyap tried to burn his son, Prahlad. Prahlad used to worship Lord Vishnu. The king did not like this. The king's sister Holika had a blessing that she could not be burnt in fire. So the king asked his sister to burn Prahlad. She sat in the fire with Prahlad. But instead of Prahlad, Holika was burnt. Holi is celebrated with colours. People throw water and 'Gulal' on one another. Children enjoy this festival most. They dance and sing and play with colours. It is difficult to recognise children's faces on this day. ●

38. Dussehra

Dussehra is an important festival of the Hindus. It is celebrated before Diwali. Lord Rama killed the demon king Ravana on this day. Dussehra gives the message that there is always victory of truth over evil. Lord Rama's life is enacted in public grounds. It is called 'Ram Lila'. Many people go to different parks to see 'Ram Lila'. It continues for ten days. On the tenth day, huge effigies of

Ravana, Kumbhakaran and Meghnad filled with crackers are erected. Then they are put to fire in a big open ground. Many people gather to see this sight. Children enjoy the fireworks and the fair. We should learn lessons from Lord Rama's life. ●

39. Independence Day

India was ruled by the Britishers before 15th August 1947. It got freedom on 15th August 1947. So this day is celebrated as Independence Day every year. On this day, in 1947, the first Prime Minister of India, Jawahar Lal Nehru hoisted the National Flag at the Red Fort and took the salute. He then delivered a message to the nation. Since then, it is celebrated every year at the Red Fort in Delhi. The Prime Minister hoists the National Flag. A salute of 21 guns is fired and the National Anthem is played. The Prime Minister delivers a message to the nation. This day is celebrated in the States and Union territories of India, in schools and other public places. ●

40. Republic Day

26th January is celebrated as Republic Day all over India every year. It was on this day in 1950 that our country became a Democratic Republic. India had a Constitution of her own. Republic Day is celebrated at India Gate in New Delhi. People come from many parts of the country to see the celebrations. The President comes to India Gate. He takes salute from the soldiers of Army, Navy and Air force. Tanks, guns and many other weapons of the armed forces are displayed. Tableaus and dancing troupes from different States pass through Raj Path. It is the most beautiful part of the celebrations. Boys and girls of different schools also take part in the procession. The parade ends at the Red Fort. In the end, there is a colourful flypast by the aeroplanes of the Indian Air Force. At night all government buildings are illuminated. ●

41. A Visit to a Zoo

Zoo is a place where different animals and birds are kept. Zoo is a great attraction for children. Last Sunday I went to see the zoo with my parents. It is situated at Purana Qila in New Delhi. We bought the tickets and went inside. Many people had already come to see the animals and birds. First of all, we saw a lion. It was grand and royal. Then we saw some tigers. Then we went to the enclosures of leopards, elephants, bears and foxes. Then we went to see the monkeys and some birds. The monkeys were jumping from one branch of the tree to another. Some monkeys were eating bananas. The birds in the zoo were very beautiful. I was very happy to see the birds. I saw some birds for the first time. Then we moved to a tank. It was full of crocodiles. We also saw some other water birds like ducks and cranes. We then saw snakes such as pythons and cobras. We spent six hours in the zoo and then came back. We enjoyed a lot in the zoo. ●

42. Politeness

Politeness is a great virtue. It costs nothing but it wins everything. If we are polite, we can win friends. We can also influence people if we are polite. Even our enemies cannot harm us if we are polite. A polite person has no enemies. Even those who are not polite are attracted by the quality of politeness. We should never lose our temper and we should always be polite to others, when we talk to them. Even when we do not like the offers and requests of others, we should turn them down politely. ●

43. Learning through Television

Television is a very useful medium of education. A lesson in the classroom is generally dull. Students find classroom lessons boring. Most of the students do not pay attention to the classroom lessons. Television creates interest among the students. It makes education an entertainment. Lessons taught through television become very interesting and they grip the attention of all the students. They remain in students' minds for a long time. Television is a good medium for mass education. The illiterate people can be educated through television. Many activities are taught to the Indian farmers through television. Through television uneducated persons can be taught about their responsibilities. Television is a good link between the masses and the government. ●

44. On being Late to School One Day

It was a cold winter morning. I was late to get out of my bed. When I got ready for the school, it was already past eight. Our school starts at 8 a.m. I did not take my breakfast. I rushed to the school. When I reached school, there was complete silence. The morning assembly was already over. The classes had started. I was in a great confusion. I thought I would get punishment. I stood at the door of my classroom. I did not know what to do. The class teacher looked at me angrily. Everybody was watching me. I was ashamed for coming late. I apologised to the teacher and she allowed me to join the class. I made up my mind to be punctual in future. ●

45. Problems of Life in Delhi

There is no doubt that life in Delhi is full of problems and hardships. Life in Delhi has many advantages also. But it can not be called a good life. There is shortage of houses. Most of the people have to live in slums. There is also the problem of conveyance. The Delhi Transport Corporation (D.T.C.) runs a large fleet of buses. But these buses are often packed to capacity. Other private buses are also overcrowded. There are taxis and auto rickshaws but one can not afford to travel by them every day. There is a lot of pollution in Delhi. Life here is very unhealthy. The houses are neither airy nor spacious. There is the problem of rising prices and scarcity of foodstuff. Life in Delhi is full of noise. There is a lot of hustle and bustle and hurry and worry. Life in Delhi may be good for a rich man but it is miserable for a poor man. ●

46. The Beggar Problem

Beggars are a very common sight in India. They can be seen in the bazaars, on the roadside, in the market places, outside cinema halls, at railway stations and at bus stops. The number of beggars is always on the increase. Some take to begging because they are very poor. Some are unemployed. Some beggars are professional beggars. They find begging a very easy way of getting money. Some beggars are handicapped and physically deformed. Some 'sadhus' are also beggars. The Indian beggar is an object of pity. Begging is also a blot on the name of India. Begging should be banned by law. Able-bodied beggars should be absorbed in suitable jobs in industries and factories. ●

47. Social Service

Man is a social animal. He cannot live alone. Society provides all comforts and necessities of life to man. Man has an obligation towards the society. Especially, it is the duty of the students to do social service to others. Students have no worries about earning their livelihood. They have strength and capacity. Eighty per cent of our population lives in villages. Students should go to the villages and serve the villagers during vacation. Villagers are illiterate, innocent and ignorant about their rights and responsibilities. Students can provide help to these people. They can also help people when there are earthquakes, famines or epidemics. Students should not waste their free time in watching movies or leading a dull life. They should do some kind of social service. ●

48. A Visit to a Village Fair

Once I visited a village on the festival of Basant. A fair was being held on the bank of a small river. I walked to the fair along with my friend. We met many villagers on the way. They were also going to see the fair. They were wearing new clothes. They looked very happy. The women were going to the fair in groups. They were singing folk songs. There was a great activity in the fair. There were shops of all kinds. There were also merry-go-rounds. We had a joy ride in them. There were rope dancers and magicians. The jugglers were also showing their tricks. There was a small temple in the fair. Many scouts were controlling the traffic. They were guiding the people and controlling the crowd. ●

49. An Excursion/Picnic

Our examinations were over. The students of our class decided to go to Okhla. It is a beautiful picnic spot. Our class teacher agreed to accompany us. We reached the school compound early in the morning. All of us had brought food in tiffin carriers and tea in flasks. We also carried other things. We started at 10 a.m. by the hired bus. We arrived at the picnic spot around at 11 a.m. We made groups and played various games. When we were tired, we ate our lunch. We were very happy in the lap of Nature. We had a nap to refresh ourselves. My friend, Suresh entertained us with his sweet songs. I told them a few anecdotes and made them laugh. We had tea and snacks. Then we enjoyed boating for some time. We left the place at 6.30 p.m. It was a nice and pleasant outing. ●

50. A Visit to a Historical Place

The schools closed for Autumn break. Our school arranged a trip to Agra. We started the next day by the Taj Express. We were very eager to see Taj Mahal. We had already read about this wonder of the world. After enjoying a comfortable journey of two hours, we reached Agra and then the historical monument, the Taj Mahal. We were spell-bound to see the beauty of the Taj. It appeared to me like a dream in marble. Shahjahan built Taj Mahal in the sweet memory of his beloved wife, Mumtaz Mahal. We saw the graves of Shahjahan and Mumtaz Mahal. Our guide explained to us each part of this monument in detail. We also paid a visit to the Red Fort of Agra and Fatehpur Sikri. We were very happy to see these historical places. This trip was very educative and entertaining. ●

51. Our School Library

Our school library is a store-house of books. It has books of different types. There are books on all subjects in our school library. Students can get any book issued in their names. Also, there are many journals and magazines in our school library. There are two big rooms. In one room there are books of science, history, literature, etc. in many languages. In this room, the books are arranged in almirahs and shelves. The other room of the library is the Reading Room. It is a quiet place. It remains open all day. Many students sit there and study. Our school librarian comes in the morning. He keeps the books in perfect order. He is very cooperative. ●

52. An Ideal School

An ideal school is situated in ideal surroundings. It is away from the noise of the city. In an ideal school there is a peaceful atmosphere. An ideal school has books of all types. Its laboratories are well-equipped. The Principal of an ideal school devotes all his time and energy to the improvement of the school. He has a team of dedicated teachers. An ideal school has arrangements for the all-round development of the students. An ideal school has large playgrounds. It encourages students to take part in extra-curricular activities. An ideal school imparts moral and religious education also. ●

53. India of My Dreams

In the India of my dreams, there will be an all-round progress. India will be at the forefront in every field. The character of her citizens will be very high. People will be honest, sincere and fair in their dealings. India of my dreams will make good progress in science and technology. Education will be free for all. No man will be illiterate. India will have a strong Army, Navy and Air Force. India will not attack any country. Nor will she tolerate any attack. The political atmosphere of the India of my dreams will be much better than what it is today. Politicians will be men of principles. Every Indian will be happy. He will make efforts to make India a strong and great nation. ●

54. Good Manners

Good manners give grace to life. They make a man a useful member of the society. Courtesy is the foundation stone of good manners. We should be courteous and polite to others. We should be soft when we talk to others. We should never lose our temper and we should be kind to others. We should give respect to our elders and teachers. We should be considerate to women and children. We should not consider ourselves superior. We should speak less and listen more. We should not hurt the feelings of any one. We should try to help everybody. Good manners cost nothing but win everything. Good manners cannot be borrowed. They are to be cultivated slowly. ●

55. Value of Games in Education

The value of games and sports is recognised by all educationists. Books develop our mind. Games develop our body. There is a sound mind in a sound body. Everybody wants to remain free from diseases. Everybody desires physical fitness. Games make our body strong. They expand our lungs and improve the blood circulation. They fill the body with strength. Games provide freshness to the mind after the day's work. Games are a good pastime also. Games and sports teach us the spirit of sportsmanship, honesty, punctuality and regularity of habits. They also teach us team spirit, leadership and obedience. Games teach us the importance of cooperative efforts and make us disciplined. They teach us how to command and how to obey. ●

56. Leisure

Leisure means free time. Leisure is a time when one is not busy in the routine work. If leisure is spent in some pleasant pursuit, it gives a great joy. Leisure gives back the lost energy to the mind. One can spend one's leisure in gardening, painting, photography, reading, rowing, stamp collecting etc. Today, man is not happy with what he has. He wants to earn more and more money. So he has no leisure. He lives in stress and strain. He suffers from many diseases such as sleeplessness, hypertension and nervous breakdown. Therefore, there is need to have leisure. One should not idle away one's leisure. Leisure has great significance in a man's life. It is only the right pursuit during leisure which can give us real happiness. ●

57. An Ideal Citizen

An ideal citizen plays an important role in the society. He thinks of his country first. He is always ready to sacrifice his own interests. He always considers himself as a member of the large society. An ideal citizen knows his rights and duties. He does not want any special favour for himself. He has great civic sense. He does not waste electricity or water. He does not misuse facilities provided to him. An ideal citizen respects the rights of others. He does not cheat the government. He does not indulge in anti-social and anti-national activities. An ideal citizen is a thorough gentleman. He is polite, courteous and very cooperative. ●

58. Annual School Function

The annual function of our school was held on 6th December. The Director of Education was the chief guest. He presided over the function and gave away the prizes. Preparations for the annual function were made a few days in advance. The school building was white-washed. The main hall was decorated. Those who were invited started coming for the function. The chief guest arrived. He was welcomed by the school Principal. He was garlanded. The Principal read out the Annual Report. The chief guest gave away prizes to brilliant students and sportsmen. He congratulated the Principal and staff on the progress made by the school. The Principal thanked the chief guest and the function came to a close with the singing of the National Anthem. ●

59. A Street Hawker

Street hawkers are found in every city. A street hawker is a mobile shop-keeper. He carries his wares on his head, bicycle or a hand cart. He sells vegetables, fruits, ice cream, toys, candies and other items of daily use. He goes from one street to another to sell his items. Some street hawkers ring bells, some make strange sounds and some sing songs to attract the attention of the customers. Housewives buy vegetables, fruits etc. from these peoples. Children buy sweets, ice-creams, toys etc. People like street hawkers because they supply things at their door steps. People bargain with them. Some hawkers are not clean. They do not cover their items from dust and flies. We should not buy eatables from such hawkers. ●

60. Advantages and Disadvantages of Science

We are living in the age of science. Television, cinema, computer, electricity, aeroplane, train, bus, telephone, mobile telephone, radio etc. are a gifts of science. From morning till evening we use things which are given to us by science. Science has given us electricity. Without electricity we cannot spend even a minute of our life. Medical science has controlled many diseases like T.B., Cholera and Small Pox. These diseases were incurable earlier. Many people used to die of these diseases. Due to scientific inventions, a lot of progress has been made in the agriculture sector. With the blessings of science, we can fly in the air and talk to a person who is sitting thousands of miles away. But science has also given us atom bombs, hydrogen bombs, nuclear bombs, tanks, missiles etc. This has raised the threat of a nuclear war. Science can be a blessing to mankind if it is used for the benefit of mankind ●

61. My Parents

The name of my father is Shri Rakesh Pandey. He is fifty-two years old. He is a teacher. He is a good person. All the students admire him. He loves his students like his own sons and daughters. He does not scold anyone. All his students respect him and worship him. He leads a simple life. He believes in simple living and high thinking. He is God-fearing and reads holy books daily. Srimati Kamla Pandey is my mother. She is a housewife. She is a very kind, religious and gentle lady. She goes to the temple daily. She also reads scriptures. She is very hard-working. She never sits idle. She cooks food for all of us. She washes our clothes and keeps the house neat and tidy. She never tells lies. I am proud of my parents.

●

62. My Best Friend

I have many friends but Ankur is my best friend. He studies in my class. We go to school together. We also sit together to do our home work. He is good at studies and helps the students who are weak in studies. Ankur is the monitor of our class. He obeys and respects his teachers and parents. He is good at games. He has won many prizes for our school. He comes from a middle-class family. His father is a teacher and his mother, a housewife. He wears clean clothes. He leads a simple life. He is always regular. He wants to become a doctor. All the teachers of our school love Ankur. I am proud of him.

●

63. My School

I am a student of Sarvodaya Vidyalaya. It is situated in Saket. My school has a two-storeyed building. There are two thousand students in my school. It has fifty rooms. All the rooms are airy and well-ventilated. Our school library has books on all subjects. Our school has a big playground. We play different games in the playground. There are forty-six teachers in my school. All the teachers are well-experienced and highly qualified. They are honest and hardworking. Shri Paswan is the Principal of our school. He is highly qualified and experienced. He is very gentle and maintains discipline in the school. Our

P.T. instructor, art and music teachers are very efficient in their fields. I am proud of my school. ●

64. My Class Teacher

I read in Manavsthali School, Kalkaji. There are about fifty teachers in my school. My class teacher, Mrs. Venu Gopal is my favourite teacher. She teaches us English. She is thirty five years old. She is an M.A. in English literature. She has done her B.Ed. also. She is the master of her subject. Her method of teaching is very interesting. Her handwriting is very neat and she has a clear voice. She loves her students like her children. She does not beat any body. She does not tolerate indiscipline in the class. She is punctual and regular. She is impartial. She does not show special favour to any student. She is very popular among the students. All the students respect and obey her. ●

65. My Classroom

I am a student of class V of Springdales School, Shanti Niketan. It has fifty classrooms. My class sits in the ground floor. I sit in room No. 38. It is near the staff room. My classroom is large. It has two doors, four ventilators and two windows. The windows have iron bars. The floor and ceiling of my classroom are cemented. There is a blackboard on the wall. The room is white-washed. There are thirty-five desks and chairs for the students. Every desk has a shelf where students keep their books and note-books. There is a armed chair and table for the teacher. There is an almirah against the wall. Our class monitor keeps the teacher's diary, chalk sticks and duster in this almirah. There are two dustbins in the classroom. There are five ceiling fans and six tubelights in the room. I like my classroom very much. ●

66. My School Principal

Mr. K.K. Sharma is the Principal of my school. He is about fifty-five years old. He is a highly qualified and experienced person. He enjoys good health. He never loses his temper. There is always a smile on his face. He wears a simple dress. He is very hardworking. He is very punctual and always comes to school on time. He inspects the classes regularly. He is a man of principles. All the students and teachers obey and respect him. He loves us like his own children. He listens to every student patiently. He takes keen interest in extra-curricular activities. We are all proud of our Principal. ●

67. My School Peon

The name of my school peon is R.R. Singh. He is thirty-eight years old. He is tall and healthy. He comes from a small village in Bihar. He is married. He lives in a small room with his wife and children. He wears a khaki uniform. He comes to school one hour before the regular school time. He cleans the Principal's room and the staff office. Then he dusts the furniture in all the classrooms. He rings the bell after a period is over. He carries the Principal's orders to the teachers. He also guides the visitors to the school. He obeys and respects all the teachers. He helps them whenever they want his help. His work is very hard. But he does all his work happily. ●

68. My House

My house is in Dwarka. It was purchased three years ago by my father. It has three bedrooms with attached bathrooms. It has a big drawing cum-dining room. It has a kitchen, a store room and a very beautiful lawn outside. The rooms of my house are spacious. They are well-ventilated. There are fans, tubes, bulbs and almirahs in all the rooms. We have a computer in our house. We also have a television set, two sofa sets, a dining table and a stereo. The kitchen has shelves, tiles and slabs. There are water taps, a geyser and shower in the bathroom. There is a garage to park our car. My house is very comfortable and I like it very much. ●

69. My School Playground

My school has a big playground. It has a huge boundary wall. We play all types of games in the playground. We play volley-ball, hockey, football, cricket and basket ball. Our school Principal encourages all students to play one or the other game. We have very strong teams of players. They practise different games in the playground. Various matches are held on this playground. The P.T. instructor of our school gives us training in the playground. He encourages all the players. Our teams have won many prizes in sports and games. Our school playground has produced many great players. They play at the national level. I am proud of my school playground. ●

70. My First Day at School

I clearly remember my first day at school. I had got admission in Nursery and went to school with my father. My father was very happy. He carried my bag and took some sweets. We went to the office of the Principal. The kind words of the Principal impressed me. Then I went to my classroom with my father. The teacher was there. He was very polite. The sweets were distributed among the children. My father shook hands with my teacher and left me there. A boy read out the lesson. All of us began repeating it. I could not learn much. But I made many friends. My teacher was very kind to me. The last bell was rung. I went back home. I was very happy. ●

71. A Prize Distribution Function

The prize distribution function of our school was held on 6th April this year. It started at 8 a.m. The whole school was decorated. The Education Minister arrived to preside over the function. He arrived at 8 a.m. The Principal received him. Teachers and students offered him bouquets of flowers. The function started with a prayer song by two girls. Then the girls staged a dance item. Then a drama was staged. All these items were liked very much. The singers and dancers were cheered. Then the Principal read out the Annual Report. It showed that the school had made good progress. The chief guest then distributed the prizes. The prize-winners received prizes and cheers. At the end, the chief guest made a short speech and congratulated the prize-winners. He advised all to work hard. The Principal thanked the chief guest. The chief guest departed. The function came to an end. ●

72. My Ambition in Life

Man is ambitious by nature. Every body has an ambition in his life. Ambition gives us aim. It gives us a sense of direction in life. My ambition is to become an ideal teacher. I can serve my people by becoming an ideal teacher. A true teacher is the builder of the nation. I shall try to mould the character of my students. I will make them ideal citizens. I shall also help them in choosing their careers. As an ideal teacher, I must have a high moral character. I shall be punctual, disciplined, humble, efficient and righteous. A good profession is its own reward. Most of the people choose a profession which can give them maximum money. My own ambition is not in this category. Wealth, power and possessions do not attract me. My aim is to serve my country. I hope I can serve my people by becoming an ideal teacher. I shall produce able citizens. This will be the greatest prize for a true and ideal teacher. ●

73. My Favourite Leader

My favourite leader is Mahatma Gandhi. He is called the 'Father of the Nation'. He was born on 2nd October, 1869 at Porbandar in Gujarat. His full name is Mohandas Karamchand Gandhi. His father, Karamchand Gandhi, was the Diwan of Rajkot. His mother Putli Bai, was a simple and religious lady. Gandhi completed his early education at Rajkot. Then he went to England. He returned to India as a barrister. He went to South Africa. He fought for the rights of the Indians living there. He left his practice as a lawyer and worked for the freedom of India. He went to jail several times. He believed in truth and non-violence. He worked for Harijans throughout his life. He worked for Hindu-Muslim unity and rural upliftment. He started movements like "Satyagrah", "Non-cooperation Movement", "Quit India Movement" and "Salt Satyagrah". He won freedom for India from the British rule on 15th August 1947. ●

74. A Cricket Match

Last Sunday our school played a cricket match against the cricket team of D.A.V. Public School. It was played on our school cricket grounds. A large number of students of both the schools witnessed the match. The P.T.I.'s of both the schools acted as umpires. There was a toss. Then the match started at 10 a.m. Our captain won the toss. He decided to bat first. Our whole team was out for 250 runs. Our captain and his opening partner scored 68 runs. The players had some refreshments during the break. Then the other team came to bat. Their batting was very strong but we bowled very well. Their captain scored 58 runs and was then bowled out. After the fall of the captain, their entire team was out for 206 runs. So we won the match by 44 runs. ●

75. A Football Match

Last Saturday our school football team played a match with Laxman Public School. It was played in our school playground. A large number of students of both the schools were present to witness the match. At 2 p.m., the teams entered the field and took their positions. After the toss, the referee blew the whistle and the match began. Our school football team played very well from the beginning. We scored four goals before half-time. After the interval, the teams changed the sides. Laxman Public School had managed to score three goals before the interval. Laxman Public School tried their best to equalise the score. The captain of Laxman Public School got the ball and scored an easy goal. The referee blew the whistle and the game came to an end. The match exciting ended in a draw. ●

76. A Hockey Match

A very interesting hockey match was played yesterday. It was played between our school team and D.A.V. School. It was played on our school playground. Many students came to see the match. The teams entered the ground at 4.45 p.m. The toss was in favour of our team. The referee blew the whistle. The match started at 5 p.m. The game was very brisk from the beginning. Our team tried their best to score a goal but they could not succeed. The Captain of D.A.V. School hit the ball and was likely to score a goal. But it was saved by our goal-keeper. The referee blew the whistle. It was interval. After the interval, the match started again. Both the teams tried their best to score goals. In the last minute of the game, D.A.V. School was given a penalty stroke. Their captain turned it into a goal. Our school team lost the match by one goal. ●

77. A House on Fire

I was asleep yesterday. Suddenly I awoke. I heard loud shouts, "Fire ! Fire !" I came out and saw that a house in our colony was on fire. The flames were rising very high. There was a thick cloud of smoke. It was a horrible sight. The fire was spreading fast. A large crowd of people had gathered. Some people were throwing buckets of water on the fire. Others were throwing sand and dust. Soon the fire brigade arrived. The firemen fought the fire bravely and brought it under control in two hours. The whole house was burnt to ashes. The loss of property was great. Luckily, there was no loss of life. ●

78. A Street Quarrel

Yesterday I heard a noise in the street. I was doing my home work then. I went out to see what had happened.

My two neighbours were quarrelling with each other. Many people had gathered to watch the quarrel. One of my neighbours had parked his car near the gate of the other neighbour. The two were not on speaking terms, so they started quarrelling. One of them started abusing. Soon both of them started exchanging hot words. The hot words were likely to change into blows. But the police van came soon. Someone had informed the police. The police head constable was an old and experienced man. He got the matter solved. He asked the neighbour to remove his car a little. This settled the matter. The quarrel came to an end. ●

79. A Stitch in Time Saves Nine

This proverb means that action taken in time can prevent many troubles. If there is a small tear in our shirt or trousers, we should mend it immediately. Otherwise, there will be need of mending many stitches. We may not be able to control the greatest loss if we do not check a small loss in the beginning. If any bad happening is not controlled in the beginning, it can lead to a greater loss and greater destruction. Those who do not care about small things in life, cannot achieve good results. Small issues grow into big problems and then one suffers. If we miss an opportunity, we cannot get it back. A small effort at the right time can save us from a greater harm. Therefore, it is essential that we do not postpone things for future but do them when needed. ●

80. Honesty is the Best Policy

It is true that honesty is the best policy. Today, we see many things around us which are not honest. Many persons are dishonest. Dishonesty may shine for some time. It may earn money, power and men. But all this is for a short time. Honesty is courageous, dishonesty is a coward. Honesty is bound to shine after the night of dishonesty. There is no place for dishonest people on the earth. They lose the battle in the end. An honest person only can win a place in the hearts of people. Double-faced men get temporary response but they are thrown out of people's hearts. Dishonesty cannot face the reality. It has to say hundred lies to hide one act of dishonesty. Therefore honesty is the best policy. ●

81. Where There is a Will There is a Way

It is a time-tested saying that where there is a will, there is a way. If we have a true desire to do something, we can find a sure way to do it. If one has a strong desire, one has to think over the details of his plan and take firm steps towards that goal. One is sure to succeed. Success will never knock our door if we keep on dreaming about it. Strong desire and courage can lead us to achieve our aim. There is nothing impossible in this world. What is needed is a strong will and right path. People who are strong-willed cannot be discouraged by failures. Strong determination is sure to bring success sooner or later. ●

82. Hostel Life

Hostel life is a free life. In a hostel, a student is free from the cares and worries of everyday. He can concentrate fully on his studies. In a hostel, a student mixes up with different types of students. He becomes well-mannered and cultured. He learns how to behave in society. He acquires good virtues and becomes a good citizen. He is able to increase his knowledge and remove his weaknesses. He interacts with other students and is no more shy. He learns to speak fluently and confidently. One should avoid bad company in a hostel. Hostel life is a memorable period of one's whole life. ●

83. Autobiography of a Rupee

I am a coin. I am called 'a rupee' by everyone. I am made of a metal. The metal has to pass through many stages in the furnaces of a mint. I had to pass through the burning fire. I play the role of a great helper. People need me badly when salary is distributed. From the highest government official to the ordinary worker, everyone needs me. I am required in every shop. If you want to buy vegetables, books, or note-books, it is essential to possess me. No one can satisfy his demands without me. Therefore I am very fortunate to help one and all. Every one wants to own me. ●

SECTION 4

LETTERS

1. *Write a letter to your uncle thanking him for the birthday gift he sent you on your birthday.*

2/3 Vasant Vihar
New Delhi

6th October 20...

My dear Uncle

I thank you very much for the camera which you sent me on my birthday. It is really a lovely present. All my friends have liked it very much.

It is very kind of you to remember me in this way on my birthday. I really needed a camera. I was planning to buy one. I am going to Agra with my friends. Now I shall be able to take photos of historical buildings.

I thank you once again for the grand present.

Please pay my regards to dear aunt.

Yours affectionately

Rohit

2. *Write a letter to your friend congratulating him on his success.*

2/292 Kailash Colony
New Delhi

23rd April 20...

Dear Rohan

I was very happy to receive your letter yesterday. We are very happy to know that you have secured 96% marks in your fifth standard examination.

We are proud of your great success. We all send you our heartiest congratulations. You have really worked hard. You deserved this success.

Please pay my regards to your parents.

Yours sincerely

Saurabh

3. ***Write a condolence letter to your friend who has lost his father.***

G-67 Saket
New Delhi

March 3, 20...

Dear Rishabh

I was greatly shocked to hear the sad news of the sudden death of your beloved father. I could not believe it. When I met him last time, he was quite healthy.

He was a very kind person. He was always helpful to others. You have to bear this loss with courage and patience. My sympathies are with you.

May God rest his soul in peace !

Yours sincerely

Ankit

4. ***Write a letter to your friend inviting him to spend his summer vacation with you.***

1229 Laxmibai Nagar
New Delhi

25th September 20...

Dear Rohan

I hope this letter finds you in the best of health and spirits.

As the summer vacation is going to start soon, I wish that you should spend a few days with us in Delhi.

There are many historical places in Delhi. You can see the Qutab Minar, Red Fort, Humayun's Tomb etc. Also, there are museums, parks and a zoo in Delhi. People come from different parts of India to see these places.

I hope you will surely spend some days of your summer vacation with us.

Convey my regards to uncle and aunt.

Yours sincerely

Puneet

5. ***Write a letter to your friend inviting him to attend your birthday party.***

C-36, C.R. Park
New Delhi

3rd January 20...

Dear Sunit

You will be glad to know that my birthday falls on 17th January. I am going to celebrate my birthday at home.

We shall have a dance and music programme. There will be a tea party at 6.30 p.m. I have invited all my friends.

I hope you will also come and join my birthday party.

Yours sincerely

Prayag

6. *Write a letter to a friend who is sick and admitted in the hospital.*

68 Anand Niketan
Bareilly

6th June 20...

Dear Suresh

I am very sorry to know that you have been lying in the hospital. Your father wrote to me that you were running high fever.

Fever is very common these days. I think your fever is due to the changing weather. I hope you will get well soon. I pray to God that you may soon recover from your sickness.

Yours sincerely

Manish

7. *Write a letter of sympathy to a friend who has failed in the examination.*

38 Malka Ganj
Agra, U.P.

June 2, 20...

Dear Gaurav

I was shocked to know that you have failed in the final examinations of fifth class.

You should not take your failure to heart. Life has successes as well as failures. Failures are the stepping stones to success.

I request you to start studying seriously again. You will pass next year with good grades. Take courage and try again.

Yours sincerely

Sonu

8. *Write a letter to your friend requesting him to lend you his camera.*

28 Roshnara Road
Delhi

27th June 20...

Dear Hari

You will be glad to know that I am going to visit Agra with my friends. If it is possible for you, please accompany us to Agra. We shall be going next week.

We want to take the photographs of all historical places at Agra. We shall also shoot the Taj Mahal.

As I do not have a camera, I request you to join us. If you cannot accompany us, please lend me your camera.

Pay my regards to your mother and father.

Yours sincerely

Rakesh

9. *Write a letter to your younger brother advising him to take part in games regularly.*

13 Anand Parbat
New Delhi

September 4, 20...

Dear Hitesh

I hope that you are doing well in your studies. There is no doubt that studies are the most important part of a student's life.

I have come to know that you do not play games. This is not good for a student. Health is wealth. Without good health you can not think of higher studies.

Games are a necessary part of education. They make us healthy and strong. I therefore advise you to take part in games and sports.

Yours sincerely

Abhishek

10. ***Write a letter to your father from the school hostel, requesting him to increase your monthly allowance.***

Lawrence School
Shimla
Himachal Pradesh

6th May 20...

My dear Father

I hope you and other members of the family are well at home. You will be glad to know that I have made good progress in my studies.

I have made very good progress in English and Mathematics. I have to purchase some books and note books. I wish to keep a tutor also.

I therefore request you to increase my monthly allowance from Rs. three hundred to Rs. four hundred from next month.

Pay my respects to mother and love to Chirag.

Your loving son

Sonu

11. ***Write a letter to your father, telling him news about your home. Your father is away from home.***

D-4 Kailash Hills
New Delhi-110048

27th December 20...

My dear Father

I am glad to inform you that all the members at home are hale and hearty. Mohan has stood first in the class.

Mother was running fever but she is all right now. She has even started attending her office now.

Everything else is fine at home.

Please write to us soon.

Your loving son

Rohit

12. ***Write a letter to your friend inviting him to your sister's marriage.***

6 West Patel Nagar
New Delhi

January 16, 20...

Dear Ankur

You will be glad to know that the marriage of my sister will be held on February 3, 20.... The marriage party will arrive from Faridabad.

We invite you and your sister to attend this marriage. Please come two days before the marriage and bring your camera also.

Yours sincerely

Saurabh

13. ***Write a letter to your friend advising him to celebrate Diwali without crackers.***

114-P Pushp Vihar
New Delh-110017

2nd November 20...

Dear Harkesh

I hope this letter finds you and the family in the best of health.

Diwali is on the 22nd of this month. I wish you and your whole family a very happy Diwali.

I advise you to celebrate Diwali without crackers. Bursting of crackers creates a lot of noise and air pollution. Crackers are also a waste of hard-earned money.

Pay my regards to uncle and aunt.

Yours lovingly

Rohit

14. ***Write a letter to your friend who has invited you to attend his birthday party, refusing the invitation.***

8/16 Gandhi Nagar
New Delhi

26th September 20...

Dear Rupesh

I was glad to receive your letter inviting me to attend your birthday party.

I am sorry to inform you that I shall not be able to attend your birthday party, as my mother is seriously ill.

Please accept my good wishes.

Yours sincerely

Ankit

15. *Write an application to the Principal of your school for granting you leave for some urgent work.*

C-33 Kailash Colony
New Delhi-110048

18th August 20...

The Principal
Senior Secondary School
Haus Khas Enclave
New Delhi-110016

Sir

With due respect I beg to say that I am not in a position to attend school. My mother is ill and there is no body else at home.

Therefore kindly grant me leave for one day viz., 19th August.

I shall be very grateful to you.

Yours obediently

Shalini Kohli
V-C

16. ***Write an application to your Principal requesting for a School Leaving Certificate and Character Certificate.***

D-84 Pamposh Enclave
New Delhi

16th July 20...

The Principal
Spring Fields School
New Delhi

Sir

I beg to inform you that I am a student of class V of your school. My father is a government servant. He has been transferred to Dehra Doon.

We are going to shift to Dehra Doon next week. Therefore kindly issue me a School Leaving Certificate and Character Certificate.

Thanking you

Yours obediently

Himanshu
V-C

17. ***Write an application to the Principal of your school for fee concession.***

C-34/A, Rohini Sector-28
New Delhi

28th March 20...

The Principal
M.R.V. School
Rohini
New Delhi
Sir

Most respectfully I beg to say that I am a student of class V of your school. My father is a clerk in a private firm.

His monthly salary is Rs. 2500. He has a large family to support.

I am good at studies and have stood first in the class. I request you to kindly grant me full fee concession. Otherwise I shall not be able to continue my studies.

Thanking you

Yours obediently

Rohit Verma
V-B

18. *Write an application to the Librarian to issue you a Duplicate Library Card.*

A-48 Dwarka
New Delhi

6th July 20...

The Librarian
Model Public School
Sector 13, Dwarka
New Delhi

Sir

This is to inform you that I lost my library card on 4th July in the school playgrounds.

The card is issued in my name and has my photo and No. 3829.

I therefore request you to cancel the above card and issue me a duplicate card.

Thanking you

Yours obediently

Raman
V-D

19. ***Write a letter to M/s ABC Publishers ordering for some books.***

38 Shastri Nagar
Meerut
U.P.

15th October 20...

The Manager
ABC Publications
Nai Sarak
Delhi

Dear Sir

I shall be highly obliged if you send me the following books by V.P.P. Kindly allow me reasonable discount.

English Grammar for Primary classes	One copy
Mathematics for Primary classes	One copy

The books should be in good condition.

Thanking you.

Yours faithfully

Subhash Chopra

20. ***Write a letter to the Postmaster complaining against the postman of your locality.***

S-34 Greater Kailash II
New Delhi-110048

26th April 20...

The Postmaster
General Post Office
New Delhi

Sir

The postman of S-Block Greater Kailash, Mr. Ram Lal is very careless. He has no sense of duty. He is never punctual.

He does not put the letters in the letter box but throws them here and there. Sometimes, he delivers the letters to the wrong persons. Sometimes he gives important letters to the children.

Kindly take some prompt action against Mr. Ram Lal.

Thanking you

Yours faithfully

Ram Prakash

21. ***Write a letter to the Health Officer drawing his attention to the insanitary conditions in your locality.***

63 Chandni Chowk
Delhi

10th August 20...

The Health Officer
Municipal Corporation of Delhi
Chandni Chowk
Delhi

Sir

I want to draw your kind attention to the insanitary conditions in our locality.

The sweeper is very careless and does not perform his duty well. Heaps of dirt and trash are lying on the road. The drains have not been cleared for many days.

Mosquitoes have started breeding. There is a fear of an outbreak of some epidemic.

I therefore request you to pay a personal visit to this area to assess the condition and take action.

Thanking you

Yours faithfully

Rakesh Ahuja

SECTION 5

COMPREHENSION

Solved Exercises

Read the following passages carefully and then answer the questions that follow :

PASSAGE 1

I wandered lonely as a cloud
That floats on high o'er vales and hills
When all at once I saw a crowd
A host of golden daffodils;
Beside the lake, beneath the trees
Fluttering and dancing in the breeze

Continuous as the stars that shine
And twinkle in the milky way,
They stretched in the never ending line
Along the margin of the bay :
Ten thousand saw I at a glance
Tossing their heads in sprightly dance

QUESTION

Exercise 1

Read the following summary of the beginning of the poem and fill in each of the spaces with one word only :

One day, the poet was .... (1) like a cloud and all of a sudden, he saw many daffodils .... (2) in the wind. He saw in one .... (3) ten thousand of them. They were .... (4) themselves sprightly.

Exercise 2

Find one word in the lines indicated which has the same meaning as each word or phrase given below : Write your answers in the space provided.

(a) a great number (lines 1 to 5) ....

(b) near (lines 2 to 6) ....

(c) under (lines 1 to 7) ....

(d) lively lines (lines 8 to 12) ....

Exercise 3

Use the following words in sentences of your own :

1. beside
2. wandered
3. breeze
4. tossing
5. fluttering

Exercise 4

Complete the Present, Past and Past Participle forms of the following verbs :

	Present	***Past***	***Past Participle***
1.	....	saw	....
2.	....	....	wandered
3.	....	stretched	....
4.	Shine	....	....
5.	....	....	floated

Exercise 5

Change the following words to Adjectives :

1. cloud
2. breeze
3. shine

ANSWERS

Exercise 1

1. wandering
2. fluttering
3. glance
4. tossing

Exercise 2

(a) host
(b) beside
(c) beneath
(d) sprightly

Exercise 3

1. Beside : She was sitting *beside* me.
2. Wandered : He *wandered* from place to place.
3. Breeze : A cool *breeze* was blowing.
4. Tossing : The saint was *tossing* his head.
5. Fluttering : The butterflies are *fluttering* their wings.

Exercise 4

Present	*Past*	*Past Participle*
1. see	saw	seen
2. wander	wandered	wandered
3. stretch	stretched	stretched
4. shine	shone	shone
5. float	floated	floated

Exercise 5

(a) cloudy
(b) breezy
(c) shiny

PASSAGE 2

Life in a big city is full of activity. Big cities have much population. People come to the cities for different aims. Big cities are centres of education, trade, business, medical facilities and industries.

People come to big cities everyday for one or the other reason. The activities start early in the morning. Everyone is busy. People come out of their homes. They go to the milk booths to fetch milk.

After sometime, long queues can be seen at bus stops. People go to their offices, shops, hospital, factories etc. Long lines of buses, cars, scooters and cycles can be seen on all the roads.

A bit city is a centre of education. Facilities of higher education and entertainment are in plenty. There are beautiful parks, hotels, clubs and roads. But people are always in hurry and worry. It is very difficult to find a house on rent. There is a lot of pollution.

QUESTIONS

Exercise 1

1. Why do big cities have much population ?

   ....

2. What do people living in the big cities do in the morning ?

   ....

3. Why do the people come to big cities every day ?

   ....

4. Describe some of the facilities which are available in big cities.

   ....

5. Describe the disadvantages of living in a big city.

   ....

Exercise 2

Put a Tick Mark (✓) against the true statement and a Cross Mark (✕) against the false statement.

1. Population in a big city is sparse. (...)
2. Life in a big city lacks in activity. (...)
3. Big cities are the centres of education and business. (...)
4. The activities in a big city start in the afternoon. (...)
5. There are many facilities in a big city. (...)
6. One can easily find a house on rent in a big city. (...)
7. A big city has no pollution. (...)

Exercise 3

Use the following words in sentences of your own :

1. activity	2. facilities	3. purpose
4. queues	5. pollution	6. worry

Exercise 4

Write the Present, Past and Past Participle forms of the following verbs.

	Present	*Past*	*Past Participle*
1.	....	....	come
2.	start	....	....
3.	....	went	....
4.	....	....	seen
5.	....	found	....

Exercise 5

A. *Change the following Nouns to Plural Number :*

1. city 2. activity 3. reason
4. queue 5. centre 6. worry

B. *Change the following words to Adjectives :*

1. population 2. education 3. reason
4. centre 5. worry

C. *Change the following words to Nouns :*

1. big 2. different 3. long
4. beautiful 5. difficult

ANSWERS

Exercise 1

1. Big cities have much population because many people come to big cities everyday for one or the other purpose.

2. In the morning, the people living in big cities go to the milk booths to fetch milk. Then they go to their offices, shops and factories.

3. People come to big cities everyday for one or the other purpose. Some come to get a job. Others come to take some medical treatment and others come for some business activity etc.

4. Some of the facilities available in the big cities are — higher education, entertainment, beautiful parks, hotels, clubs and roads.

5. People living in a big city lead a life of hurry and worry. There is a lot of pollution in a big city.

Exercise 2

1. (✗) 2. (✗) 3. (✓) 4. (✗) 5. (✓)
6. (✗) 7. (✗)

Exercise 3

1. There is a lot of *activity* in all big cities.
2. There are many *facilities* in this hotel.
3. What is the *purpose* of your visit ?
4. There were long *queues* at the bus stops.
5. Big cities are full of *pollution*.
6. He has no *worry*.

Exercise 4

Present	*Past*	*Past Participle*
1. come	came	come
2. start	started	started
3. go	went	gone
4. see	saw	seen
5. find	found	found

Exercise 5

A. 1. cities 2. activities 3. reasons
4. queues 5. centres 6. worries

B. 1. populous 2. educational 3. reasonable
4. central 5. worried

C. 1. bigness 2. difference 3. length
4. beauty 5. difficulty

PASSAGE 3

India is a country of villages. There are more than five lakh villages in India. Eighty per cent of India's population lives in villages. The village people are uneducated, ignorant and backward.

There is poverty in villages. The villagers do not have proper means to make progress. It is the duty of the young people of India to help the villagers. They should go to the villages and help the people living there.

The roads in the villages are dusty. Many people live in huts. There is no proper drainage system there. Most of the adults are uneducated. They do not take part in national programmes. The villagers should be taught how to read and write. They should be taught about the advantages of a small family.

QUESTIONS

Exercise 1

1. Where does most of India's population live ?

   ....

2. What are the problems of the people living in the villages ?

   ....

3. What is the duty of the young people of India ?

   ....

4. What should the villagers be taught ?

   ....

Exercise 2

Complete the following sentences :

1. There are more than .... in India.

2. India's .... population lives in villages.

3. The villagers have the following problems.

   (i) There is poverty in the villages.

   (ii) ....

4. The young people should

   (i) .... living there.

5. The roads in the villages are ....

6. Many people live ....

7. The villagers should be taught

   (i) ....

   (ii) about the advantages of a small family.

Exercise 3

A. *Write the Past and Past Participle forms of the following verbs* :

1. have 2. make 3. help
4. live 5. take 6. read
7. write

B. *Change the following words to Abstract Nouns* :

1. uneducated 2. ignorant 3. backward

C. *Change the following words to Adjectives* :

1. help 2. progress 3. family

D. *Use the following words in sentences of your own* :

1. population 2. backward 3. duty
4. help 5. proper 6. advantages

ANSWERS

Exercise 1

1. Most of India's population lives in villages.

2. There is poverty in the villages. The villagers do not have proper means to make progress. The roads and dusty. Many villagers live in huts.
3. The duty of the young people of India is to help the villagers. They should go to the villages and help the people living there.
4. The villagers should be taught how to read and write. They should be taught about the advantages of a small family.

Exercise 2

1. five lakh villages
2. eighty per cent
3. (ii) The villagers do not have proper means to make progress.
4. (i) help the people
5. dusty
6. in huts
7. (i) how to read and write

Exercise 3

	Present	*Past*	*Past Participle*
A.	have	had	had
	make	made	made
	help	helped	helped
	live	lived	lived
	take	took	taken
	read	read	read
	write	wrote	written

B. 1. uneducation 2. ignorance 3. backwardness

C. 1. helpful 2. progressive 3. familial

D. 1. The *population* of India is increasing rapidly.
2. Bangladesh is a *backward* country.
3. It is our *duty* to obey the laws.
4. We should *help* the poor.
5. You should take *proper* diet.
6. What are the *advantages* of science ?

PASSAGE 4

The farmers sow their crops and reap the harvests. There are sowing seasons and harvesting seasons in rural India. As the crops grow, the farmers' hearts leap with joy. They expect to gather the fruit of their labour. The farmers employ a large force of landless labourers. These labourers cut the crops and get their wages.

When the crop is ready for sickle, they start the work of harvesting it. All of them move down to the fields with beaming faces. They start their work early in the morning. They swiftly go on reaping their crops and they laugh and sing. They enjoy their work. Thus, the gay field turns into a deserted field.

QUESTIONS

Exercise 1

Answer the following questions as briefly as possible :

1. What do the farmers do ?

    ....

2. What seasons are there in rural India ?

    ....

3. Why do the farmers employ a large force of landless labourers ?

    ....

4. When do the farmers start their work of harvesting ?

   ....

5. How does the field look after harvesting ?

   ....

Exercise 2

Put a Tick Mark (✓) against the true statement and a Cross Mark (X) against the false statement.

1. The farmers sow their crops and cut the crops when they are ripe. (...)
2. There are sowing seasons and harvesting seasons in urban India. (...)
3. The farmers expect to gather the fruit of their labour. (...)
4. The farmers do the harvesting by themselves. (...)
5. Farmers start harvesting soon after they have sown the field. (...)
6. The farmers laugh and sing when they cut their crops. (...)

Exercise 3

Complete the following blanks :

1. There are two types of seasons in rural India :
   (i) sowing seasons and
   (ii) ....
2. As the crops grow, the farmers' hearts .... joy.
3. When the crop is ready .... (i) they start the work of .... (ii).

4. The farmers reap their crops and they
   (i) laugh
   (ii) ....
   (iii) ....

Exercise 4

A. *Write the Antonyms (opposite meanings) of the following words :*

1. rural 2. joy 3. start
4. down 5. early

B. *Use the following words in sentences of your own :*

1. get 2. crop 3. work
4. move 5. fruit 6. employ

C. *Change the following words to Nouns :*

1. employ 2. expect 3. grow
4. move 5. ready

D. *Change the following words to Adjectives :*

1. joy 2. fruit 3. force
4. laugh

ANSWERS

Exercise 1

1. The farmers sow their crops and reap the harvests.
2. There are sowing seasons and harvesting seasons in rural India.
3. The farmers employ a large force of landless labourers to harvest their fields.
4. The farmers start their work of harvesting when the crop is ready for sickle.
5. The field looks deserted after harvesting.

Exercise 2

1. (✓) 2. (✗) 3. (✓) 4. (✗) 5. (✗)
6. (✓)

Exercise 3

1. (ii) harvesting seasons
2. leap with
3. (i) for sickle (ii) harvesting it
4. (ii) sing and (iii) enjoy their work

Exercise 4

A. 1. urban 2. sorrow 3. stop
4. up 5. late

B. 1. You should *get* your salary in time.
2. The *crop* is ready for harvesting.
3. You should *work* hard.
4. Do not *move* forward.
5. Hard work brings *fruit*.
6. He will *employ* a peon for his office.

C. 1. employment 2. expectation 3. growth
4. movement 5. readiness

D. 1. joyful 2. fruitful 3. forceful
4. laughable

Unsolved Exercises For Practice

PASSAGE I

Read the following passage carefully and answer the questions that follow :

An ideal student should have many qualities. He should follow a regular code of conduct. He should get up early in the morning and take care of his health.

A good student should take a morning walk every day. He should wear clean and smart clothes. He should reach school in time. He should complete his home work and class work. He should have sweet and lovable habits. At home, he should respect his parents.

An ideal student should be humble and polite. He should talk less and work more. He should show respect to the teachers.

QUESTIONS

Exercise 1

Answer the following questions as briefly as possible in your own words :

1. What type of clothes should a good student wear ?

   ....

2. What type of habits should a good student have ?

   ....

3. To whom should an ideal student show respect ?

   ....

4. Describe any three qualities of a good student.

   ....

   ....

   ....

Exercise 2

Fill in the blanks in the following sentences :

1. An ideal student should follow a .... conduct.

2. An ideal student should get up early in the morning and .... health.

3. A good student should take a morning ....

4. An ideal student should be

(i) ....

(ii) and polite

Exercise 3

A. *Use the following words in sentences of your own :*

1. qualities	2. regular	3. health
4. reach	5. habits	6. respect

B. *Change the following words to Nouns :*

1. regular	2. clean	3. complete
4. lovable	5. polite	6. sweet

C. *Change the following words to Antonyms (having opposite meanings) :*

1. many	2. regular	3. clean
4. sweet	5. respect	6. polite

D. *Fill in the blanks with appropriate forms of the words given in brackets :*

1. An ideal student should follow a .... code of conduct. (regularity)
2. A good student should have sweet and .... habits. (love)
3. An ideal student should be humble and .... (politeness)
4. An ideal student should take care of his .... (healthy)

PASSAGE 2

Read the following passage carefully and answer the questions that follow :

We see street hawkers everyday. They are found in every city. A street hawker is a mobile shop-keeper. He carries his wares on his head, on a cycle or a hand cart.

He sells all kinds of things such as vegetables, fruit, ice cream, eatables, balloons, toys and many other things of daily use. He goes from one street to another to sell his wares. He shouts in the street in an interesting tone.

His customers are housewives who buy vegetables, fruit etc. Children buy toys, ice-cream, sweets etc. from a street hawker. A street hawker has no fixed price. People bargain with him before buying.

QUESTIONS

Exercise 1

Answer the following questions as briefly as possible in your own words. Write the answers in the space provided :

1. How does a street hawker carry his wares ?

   ....

2. What kind of things does a street hawker sell ?

   ....

3. Who are the customers of a street hawkers ?

   ....

4. What do the housewives buy from a street hawker ?

   ....

5. What do people do before buying things from a street hawker ?

....

Exercise 2

Put a Tick Mark (✓) against the true statement and a Cross Mark (X) against the false statement :

1. Street hawkers are found in all the villages of India. (...)
2. A street hawker sells his things while moving from one place to another. (...)
3. He carries his things in an auto rickshaw. (...)
4. The customers of a street hawker are grown up men. (...)
5. Children do not buy anything from a street hawker. (...)
6. Street hawkers are found in all cities. (...)
7. People do not bargain with a street hawker before buying things. (...)
8. A street hawker sells vegetables, fruit, ice-cream, balloons, toys. etc. (...)

Exercise 3

Fill in the following blanks with suitable words :

1. Street hawkers are found in .... city.
2. A street hawker is a .... shopkeeper.
3. A street hawker carries his things on
   (i) his head
   (ii) ....
   (iii) ....

4. He sells
   (i) vegetables
   (ii) ....
   (iii) ....
   (iv) ....
   (v) toys
5. The customers of a street hawker are :
   (i) ....
   (ii) children
6. A street hawker has no .... price.

Exercise 4

A. *Change the following words to Nouns :*

1. mobile 2. interesting 3. buy
4. carries

B. *Use the following words in sentences of your own :*

1. shop-keeper 2. wares 3. another
4. mobile 5. see 6. bargain

C. *Change the following words to Antonyms/having opposite meanings :*

1. everyday 2. mobile 3. sells
4. interesting 5. buy 6. before

PASSAGE 3

Read the following passage carefully and answer the questions that follow :

Once there was a hunter. He lived in a village. He had a dog. It was very faithful. One day the hunter went to the city with his wife. He left his son at home under the guard of the dog.

A wolf came there. He entered the house and attacked the son. The dog fought with the wolf and killed it. In the evening, the hunter and his wife returned from the city. The dog was waiting outside the house for its master. When he saw his master, he licked his feet. The hunter saw blood on the face of the dog. He thought that the dog had killed his son. He took his gun and killed the dog.

When he found his son safe inside the house, he wept bitterly.

QUESTIONS

Exercise 1

Answer the following questions as briefly as possible in your own words :

1. Where did the hunter live ?

   ....

2. With whom did the hunter go to the city ?

   ....

3. With whom did the hunter leave his son ?

   ....

4. What did the wolf do ?

   ....

5. What did the dog do when the wolf entered the house ?

   ....

6. Why did the hunter kill his faithful dog ?

   ....

Exercise 2

Put a Tick Mark (✓) against the true statement and a Cross Mark (X) against the false statement :

1. The dog of the hunter was very faithful. (...)
2. The hunter went to the city with his wife and son. (...)
3. The hunter left his son in the care of his dog. (...)
4. The wolf killed the hunter's dog. (...)
5. The dog fought with the wolf and killed it. (...)
6. The hunter and his wife did not return from the city for two days. (...)
7. When the dog saw his master, he licked his feet. (...)
8. The hunter thought that wolf had killed his son. (...)
9. The hunter thought that the dog had killed his son. (...)
10. The hunter wept bitterly on finding his son safe. (...)

Exercise 3

Fill in the blanks in the following sentences :

1. One day the hunter went to the city with his ....
2. He left his son at home under the .... of his ....
3. A wolf who came there

   (i) entered the house

   (ii) ....

4. The hunter and his wife returned from the city ....

5. The dog was waiting outside the house ....

6. The hunter saw .... on the face of the ....

7. The hunter thought that the dog .... son

8. When the hunter found his son safe inside the house .... bitterly.

Exercise 4

A. *Change the following words to Nouns :*

1. entered 2. fought 3. safe
4. faithful 5. bitterly

B. *Change the following words to Adjectives :*

1. blood 2. face 3. bitterly

C. *Use the following words in sentences of your own :*

1. lived 2. village 3. faithful
4. fought 5. hunter 6. inside

D. *Change the following sentences into Present Tense :*

1. A wolf came there.
2. He entered the house.
3. The dog fought with the wolf and killed it.
4. He took his gun and killed the dog.
5. When he found his son safe inside the house, he wept bitterly.

E. *Write the Antonyms of the following words :*

1. went 2. faithful 3. attacked
4. safe 5. inside 6. bitterly

PASSAGE 4

It was a hot summer day. A wolf felt thirsty. He went to a stream to drink water. When he was drinking water, he saw a lamb. It was drinking water down the stream.

The wolf wanted to eat the lamb. He said, "Lamb, why are you making the water dirty ?" The poor lamb said, "Sir, the water is flowing from you to me. How can I make it dirty". After a few minutes, the wolf said, "Why did you abuse me last year ?" The lamb said, "I was not born last year." "Then it must have been your father or mother. I will not forgive you", the wolf said, and tore the lamb to pieces and ate it up.

QUESTIONS

Exercise 1

Answer the following questions as briefly as possible in your own words. Write your answers in the space provided.

1. Why did the wolf go to a stream ?

   ....

2. What was the lamb doing in the stream ?

   ....

3. What did the wolf want ?

   ....

4. What did the wolf say to the lamb for the first time ?

   ....

5. What did the wolf say to the lamb for the second time ?

   ....

6. What were the replies of the lamb ?

....

7. What did the wolf do to the lamb in the end ?

....

Exercise 2

Put a Tick Mark (✓) against the true statement and a Cross Mark (✗) against the false statement :

1. A wolf was feeling thirsty on a hot summer day. (...)
2. A lamb was drinking water down the stream. (...)
3. The wolf did not want to eat the lamb. (...)
4. The wolf asked the lamb why he was making the water dirty. (...)
5. The water was flowing from the wolf to the lamb. (...)
6. The water was flowing from the lamb to the wolf. (...)
7. The wolf told the lamb that his (lamb's) father must have made the water dirty. (...)
8. The wolf felt pity on the lamb. (...)
9. The wolf ate the lamb up. (...)
10. The wolf was a cruel animal. (...)
11. The wolf was a kind animal. (...)

Exercise 3

A. *Change the following words to Nouns :*

1. hot 2. dirty 3. poor
4. forgive 5. thirsty

B. *Use the following words in sentences of your own :*

1. hot	2. thirsty	3. stream
4. dirty	5. flowing	6. forgive

C. *Write the Antonyms of the following words :*

1. hot	2. dirty	3. poor
4. forgive	5. last	6. after

PASSAGE 5

Many festivals are celebrated in India. Deepawali is one of them. It is an important festival. Deepawali means 'rows of lights'.

On this day, Lord Rama, Lakshmana and Sita returned to Ayodhya after 14 years of exile. People lighted earthen lamps to greet them. They decorated the city to express their joy.

On this day, people clean their houses and shops and get them whitewashed. They decorate their houses. People exchange gifts and sweets. In the evening, people illuminate their houses. Lamps and candles are placed in every corner of the house. Children burst fire crackers. These fire crackers pollute the atmosphere.

QUESTIONS

Exercise 1

Answer the following questions as briefly as possible in your own words. Write the answers in the space provided.

1. What is the meaning of Deepawali ?

   ....

2. What happened on this day ?

   ....

3. Why did people light earthen lamps ?

....

4. What do people do on this day ?

....

5. What do people exchange on Deepawali ?

....

6. How do children celebrate Deepawali ?

....

Exercise 2

Put a Tick Mark (✓) against the true statement and a Cross Mark (✕) against the false statement :

1. Very few festivals are celebrated in India. (...)
2. Deepawali means 'rows of lights'. (...)
3. On this day Lord Rama, Lakshmana and Sita returned to Ayodhya after forty years of exile. (...)
4. People lighted electric lamps to celebrate the return of Lord Rama and others. (...)
5. On Deepawali, lamps and candles are placed in every corner of the house. (...)
6. Fire crackers pollute the atmosphere. (...)
7. Therefore, children do not burst fire crackers. (...)

Exercise 3

Fill in the blanks in the following sentences :

1. Many .... are celebrated in India.
2. Deepawali means .... lights.

3. Lord Rama, Lakshmana and Sita returned to Ayodhya after .... of exile.
4. People decorated Ayodhya to .... joy.
5. On this day people clean their
   (i) ....
   (ii) and shops
6. People exchange
   (i) gifts
   (ii) and ....
7. Children burst .... on this day.
8. Fire crackers .... atmosphere.

Exercise 4

A. *Change the following words to Nouns :*

1. celebrate	2. important	3. greet
4. illuminate	5. pollute	6. decorate

B. *Use the following words in sentences of your own :*

1. festivals	2. important	3. greet
4. exchange	5. illuminate	6. crackers

C. *Change the following sentences into Present tense :*

1. People lighted earthen lamps.
2. They decorated the city to express their joy.

D. *Change the following sentences into Past tense :*

1. On this day people clean their houses and shops.
2. People exchange gifts and sweets.
3. These fire crackers pollute the atmosphere.
4. People illuminate their houses.

SECTION 6

STORIES

1. The Greedy Dog

Outline : *A hungry dog — wandered here and there — found a piece of meat — crossed the bridge — saw shadow in the water — another dog — barked at another dog — own piece of meat fell down — realised his foolishness.*

Once there lived a dog. He was very hungry. He wandered here and there in search of food. He got a piece of meat from a butcher's shop. He took the piece of meat and ran away. He reached a river bridge. He saw his own shadow in the water. He thought that there was another dog with a bigger piece of meat in his mouth. His mouth watered. He wanted to snatch the piece of meat from him. He barked at him. As he opened his mouth, his own piece of meat fell into the water.

Moral : *Greed is a curse*

2. A Wolf and the Shepherd Boy

Outline : *A village boy — daily takes sheep out for grazing — one day thinks of mischief — climbs up a tree and shouts — wolf coming — people rush to help him — no wolf — the boy laughs at them — another day the same thing — one day a wolf comes — the boy shouts — people don't believe — boy is eaten up — moral.*

Once there lived a boy. He lived in a small village. He took out his sheep for grazing every day. He would go to a nearby jungle. One day he thought of a mischief. He climbed up a tree and shouted, "Help ! Help ! A wolf is coming". The villagers rushed to his help. They found no wolf there. The boy laughed at them. He said that he had cried for the sake of fun. The villagers went back. On another day, he repeated the joke. The villagers again came to help him. They found no wolf. One day a wolf actually came there. The boy shouted for help. No one came to his help. The wolf killed him and his sheep also.

Moral : *Once a liar, always a liar.*

3. The Lion and the Mouse

Part of a story is given below : you have to complete it.

Once a lion was sleeping in a jungle. He was woken up by a mouse. The lion became angry. The mouse pleaded for his life. He promised to help the lion. The lion let it go. Once the lion got caught in a trap ......

Once there lived a lion. He was sleeping under a shady tree. A mouse lived in a hole nearby. It came out of its hole. It began to move up and down on the body of the lion. The lion woke up from his sleep. He was very angry. He wanted to kill the mouse. The mouse prayed for its life. It said, "Please spare my life. I will pay back your kindness". The lion took pity and set the mouse free.

One day, the lion was caught in a net. He began to roar. The little mouse heard his roar and came there. It saw the lion caught in a net. It cut the net with its sharp teeth. The lion was free. He thanked the little mouse for its timely help.

Moral : *Do good and have good.*

4. Bad Company

Outline : *An old man — four sons — mixed with bad boys — advised — no effect — basket full of mangoes — a rotten mango — all mangoes were rotten — a lesson.*

Once there was an old man. He had four sons. They had fallen into bad company. They mixed up with gamblers. The father advised them not to mix with such persons. But the advice had no effect on them. One day, the old man bought a basketful of mangoes. He told the sons to eat the mangoes the next morning.

The old man kept one rotten mango among them. The next morning, the sons found that most of the mangoes were rotten. The father told them the cause. The sons learnt a lesson. They left the bad company.

Moral : *A single rotten mango can spoil all others.*

5. The Hidden Treasure

Outline : *An old farmer was about to die — his five sons — lazy — he told them about the treasure in his fields — sons dug all around — no treasure — good crop — a lesson.*

A farmer had five sons. They were all lazy. The farmer wanted to see them as hard-working young men. He was worried about their future. One day he fell ill. He was on his death-bed. He called his sons. He told them that there was a treasure hidden in his fields. He passed away the same day.

The sons went to the fields. They dug up every inch of the fields. They did not find the hidden treasure. After a few days, it rained heavily. Some one advised them to sow seeds in the fields. They did the same. They got a good crop. They became rich. Now they understood the value of hard work. They got the hidden treasure from the fields in the form of good crops.

Moral : *No pains no gains*

or

Work is its own reward.

6. The Farm Dog and the Wolf

Outline : *A wolf meets a farm dog — wolf very thin — dog advises — "Do honest work — master feeds well" — wolf agrees — notices marks round dog's neck — "why"? — mark of chain — wolf refuses to work — rather to remain free and starve.*

Once there was a wolf. He came to a farm. He met the farm dog. The dog was quite healthy. The wolf was thin. The wolf asked him the secret of his health. The dog replied that he kept watch over the farm and his master fed him well. The dog advised him, "Do work honestly and the master will feed you well". The wolf agreed.

The wolf noticed some marks round the dog's neck. He asked the dog about it. The dog replied that during the day he had to wear the chain round his neck. The wolf was shocked to hear this. He said, "I would rather be free and starve than be a slave to any body".

Moral : *Better be hungry than in chains.*

7. The Cap-seller and the Monkeys

Outline : *Cap-seller — sell caps — village market — forest — basket of red caps — tired — put basket on ground — fell asleep — monkeys in tree — took caps — plan — threw caps on ground — Moral.*

Once a cap-seller was going to sell his caps in a village market. He was going through a forest. He was carrying a basket of red caps on his head. He got tired in the heat of the sun. He lay down under a tree to take rest. He put his basket on the ground. He fell asleep.

There were monkeys on that tree. They came down and took the caps. Then they climbed on the tree. When the cap-seller woke up, he was surprised to see that monkeys were wearing his caps. He became sad. He thought of a plan. He threw his own cap on the ground. The monkeys also threw down their caps. He collected his caps and went away.

Moral : *Wit works where strength fails.*

8. A Thirsty Crow

Outline : *A hot summer day — no water — a crow very thirsty — flew in search of water — sees pitcher with some water — tries to drink — low level — drops pebbles — level rises — quenches his thirst.*

It was a hot summer day. A crow was very thirsty. He flew here and there in search of water. He could not find the water. He sat on a branch of a tree. There was a pitcher under the tree. There was some water in the pitcher. He was very happy to see the pitcher.

He tried to drink water but the level of water was low. His beak could not reach the water in the pitcher. He thought of a plan. He dropped some pebbles in the pitcher, one by one. The level of water rose up. The crow drank the water and flew away.

Moral : *Where there is a will, there is a way.*

9. Union is Strength
or
United We Stand

Outline : *An old farmer — had five sons — selfish — quarrelled with one another — farmer on death bed — wanted to teach them a lesson — asked his servant to bring a bundle of sticks — called his sons one by one — asked them to break — in vain — untie the bundle — each breaks — a bundle stronger than the stick — lesson from the story.*

Once there was an old farmer. He had five sons. They were very selfish. They always quarrelled with one another. He was worried about them. When he was on his death bed, he wanted to teach them a lesson. He advised them to live in unity. But they did not care.

He asked his servant to bring a bundle of sticks. Then he called his sons one by one and asked them to break the bundle. But no one could do that. Then he ordered the servant to untie the bundle. Now each one of them could break the sticks easily. He advised his sons to live like a bundle of sticks. If they quarrelled, the people would harm them. The sons promised to live unitedly.

Moral : *Union is strength.*

10. The Fox and the Grapes

Outline : *A hungry fox — jumps at grapes — they were too high — tired — gave up the attempt — called grapes sour.*

Once there was a fox. He was hungry. He went in search of food. He could not find any food. At last he reached a vineyard. Bunches of grapes were hanging. He wanted to get them. His mouth began to water. The grapes were very high. He tried to get at the grapes. He jumped again and again. But all his efforts were useless. The grapes were too high for him to reach. He got tired. He was sure that he could not get the grapes. He gave up the attempt. He went away saying that the grapes were sour.

Moral : *The grapes are sour if they are not within reach.*

11. The Fox and the Crow

Outline : *A fox in a forest — hungry — a crow with a piece of bread on the tree — he praises the crow — the crow sings — the fox runs away with his piece of bread.*

Once there was a fox. He was hungry. He ran in search of food but could not find anything to eat. He saw a crow sitting on the branch of a tree. It had a piece of bread in its beak. His mouth watered. He thought of a plan. He praised the crow for its sweet songs. He prayed to him to sing a song. The crow felt proud. As the crow opened its mouth to sing, its own piece of bread fell down. The fox took it away and ate it.

Moral : *Beware of flatterers.*

12. An Honest Woodcutter

Outline : *A poor woodcutter cutting trees in the forest — axe falls into the river — river deep — weeps — god Mercury appears — brings a golden axe — woodcutter refuses — refuses to take silver axe — agrees to take iron axe — god pleased — rewards him.*

Once there lived a poor woodcutter. He used to cut trees in the woods. One day he was cutting wood on the bank of a river. His axe fell down into the river. The river was deep. He could not take his axe out. He sat on the bank and began to weep.

Mercury, the god of water appeared. He asked the reason of his weeping. The woodcutter told the whole story. Mercury dived into the water and brought a golden axe. The woodcutter refused to take it. Mercury again dived and brought a silver axe. The woodcutter did not take it either. Then he brought an iron axe. The woodcutter took it gladly. Mercury was much pleased. He rewarded the woodcutter with the other two axes.

Moral : *Honesty is the best policy.*

13. King Bruce and the Spider

Outline : *Bruce defeated — becomes disappointed — runs away from the battle field — hides in a cave — sees a spider trying to reach the roof — fails many times — succeeds in the last attempt.*

Once upon a time there was a king in Scotland. His name was Robert Bruce. He fought many battles. Once he was defeated. He ran away from the battle field. He hid himself in a cave. There was a spider in that cave. It was trying to reach the roof of the cave. It failed again and again. After every fall, the spider tried again. It did not lose heart. The spider reached its web in the seventh attempt.

The spider taught King Bruce a great lesson. It filled him with new hope and courage. He came out of the cave and gathered his forces. This time he fought bravely. He was successful in making his country free.

Moral : *Try, try again till you succeed.*

14. The Salt Merchant and His Ass

Outline : *A salt merchant — loads his ass with salt — ass falls into the river — load becomes lighter — next time it falls purposely — loaded with cotton — ass could not walk due to heavy load — a lesson.*

Once there was a merchant. He had an ass. He always overloaded it with salt. The load was very heavy for it. One day it fell down into the river while crossing it. When it came out of the water, the load became lighter. The ass felt happy. Next day, the ass fell into the river knowingly. The merchant understood its trick. He decided to teach it a lesson.

Next time he loaded the ass with cotton. The ass repeated the trick. The cotton became wet and very heavy. It came out of water with great difficulty. The merchant gave it a good beating. The ass learnt a lesson. It never repeated the trick.

Moral : *Cleverness does not pay always.*

15. The Wolf and the Lamb

Outline : *A lamb was drinking water — a hungry wolf reached — wanted to eat it — blamed for making water muddy — the lamb proved his innocence — abused last year — not born — killed the lamb — ate it up — Moral.*

Once upon a time, a lamb was drinking water on the bank of a river. A hungry wolf reached there. The wolf's mouth began to water. He wanted to eat the lamb. He shouted at the lamb, "Why are you making the water muddy?" The lamb replied, "Sir, the water is coming from your side". Then the wolf said, "Why did you abuse me last year ?" "I was not born last year", replied the lamb. The wolf grew angry. He said, "Your father might have abused me". Saying these words, the wolf killed the lamb and ate it up.

Moral : *Might is right.*

16. The Sun and the Wind

Outline : *Dispute between sun and wind who is stronger — sees a traveller — whosoever makes the traveller take off his coat — wind blows hard — turn of sun — sun shines brightly — takes off his coat — the sun wins.*

Once a dispute arose between the sun and the wind. Each thought that it was stronger than the other. It was decided whosoever made the traveller take off his coat, would be stronger than the other. The wind blew harder and harder. The traveller felt cold. He held on his coat tightly. Now it was the turn of the sun. The sun grew hotter and hotter. The traveller took off his coat. Thus the sun won.

Moral : *Boasters, like the wind, lick dust.*

17. The Slave and the Lion

Outline : *A slave runs away from his cruel master — sees a cave in the forest — lion comes — pulls out a thorn from his paw — friendship — slave was caught — thrown before a hungry lion — does not eat him — set free.*

Once there was a slave in Rome. His master was very cruel. He ran away to a forest. He went into a cave to live there. He slept in the cave. Suddenly he woke up to hear the roar of a lion. He saw a lion there. The lion was limping. The slave saw a thorn in the lion's paw. He pulled it out. The lion felt relief. Both became friends.

One day, the slave was caught by his master's men. He ordered him to be thrown before a hungry lion. When the slave was brought before the lion, the lion did not kill him. It was the same lion. The lion licked his feet. All were surprised at this strange sight. The slave was set free. The lion was given to him as a reward.

Moral : *Kindness never goes unrewarded.*

18. The Hare and the Tortoise

Outline : *A hare and a tortoise — hare proud of his speed — race started — passes by the sleeping hare — reaches the goal — hare wakes up — in vain.*

Once there lived in a forest a hare and a tortoise. The hare was very proud of his speed. He made fun of the tortoise for his slow speed. The tortoise challenged the hare to have a race with him. The hare accepted the challenge.

The race started. The crow was the referee. The hare ran very fast. The tortoise was left much behind. The hare stopped to take rest under a tree. He fell asleep. The tortoise passed him and reached the winning post. The hare woke up and ran as fast as he could. He saw that the tortoise was already there at the winning post. He had won the race.

Moral : *Slow and steady wins the race*

or

Pride hath a fall.

19. The Faithful Dog

Outline : *Dark night — perfect silence — family lay in sound sleep — fire broke out — the dog barked —young child left inside — dog rushed — all praised the dog.*

Once there lived a man in the village. He had a dog. It was very faithful. One night, the family was sleeping in a room. Suddenly a fire broke out. The flames were rising high. The dog barked and barked. All the members of the family woke up. They ran out to save their lives. A young child was left inside. Flames were rising in the sky. Nobody was ready to risk his life. The dog rushed into the flames. He himself was burnt but caught the child. He brought the child out of the house. All were happy. The master patted the dog. All praised the dog for the great act that saved the child's life.

Moral : *Faithfulness is always rewarding.*

20. The Hare and the Lion

Outline : *Lion — king of the forest — kills many animals — animals offer to serve him — another lion — lion wants to see — deep well — lion sees his reflection — jumps in and dies — animals happy.*

Once there lived a lion in the forest. He was the king of the animals. He killed many animals. The animals were in terror. They held a meeting. An old hare stood up. He was wise. He brought forth a plan. All the animals went to the lion. The animals told him that they would send one animal every day. The lion agreed.

One day, it was the hare's turn. He reached the lion late. The lion was angry. He asked the hare why he was late. The hare said that another lion had held him on the way. The lion told him to show the other lion. The hare led him to a deep well. The lion looked into the well and saw his own image in the water. He took his image for another lion. He at once jumped into the well and died. The animals lived happily after that.

Moral : *Wisdom is stronger than strength.*

21. Two Friends and the Bear

Outline : *Forest — two travellers — meet bear — one climbs up a tree — the other lies down as if dead — bear smells his body — goes away.*

Mohan and Sohan were friends. They lived in a village. Once they made a plan to go to Varanasi. They passed through a forest. Wild animals lived in that forest.

On the way, they saw a bear. Sohan was selfish. He climbed up a tree to save his life. Mohan could not climb up the tree. He lay down on the ground. He held his breath. The bear smelt him and took him to be dead. He went away. Sohan came down. He asked Mohan "What was the bear speaking in your ears ?" Mohan replied, "He advised me to beware of those friends who run away in time of danger".

Moral : *A friend in need is a friend indeed.*

22. The Stag and his Horns

Outline : *A stag with beautiful horns — sees his reflection in water — admires his horns — ashamed of his thin legs — hears the sound of hunter's dogs — runs away — legs help him — horns get entangled in a bush — the dogs kill him.*

Once a stag was drinking water in a pool. He saw the reflection of his horns in the water. He felt proud. When he saw the reflection of his legs, he felt ashamed. Just then, he heard the barking of a hunter's dogs. He ran away as fast as he could. His thin legs helped him to escape. He realised that his ugly-looking legs were his real friends.

Soon his beautiful horns proved an enemy to him. They got entangled in a bush. He tried his best to release himself. But he could not succeed. The dogs reached there. They killed him.

Moral : *All that glitters is not gold.*

23. A Faithful Dog and Its Master

Outline : *A hunter had a faithful dog — leaves to town — dog guards the baby — a wolf — dog kills it — hunter sees the blood stains — kills the dog — baby safe — weeps bitterly.*

Once there was a hunter. He lived in a village. He had a dog. It was very faithful. One day, the hunter went to the city with his wife. He left his son at home. A wolf came there. It entered the house and attacked the baby. The dog fought with the wolf and killed it.

In the evening, the hunter and his wife returned from the city. The dog was waiting outside for its master. When it saw its master, he licked its feet. The hunter saw the stains of blood on the dog's mouth. He thought that the dog had killed his son. He became very angry. He took his gun and killed the dog. When he found his son safe inside the house and the wolf lying dead near him, he wept bitterly.

Moral : *Haste makes waste.*

24. The Fisherman and His Partner

Outline : *A king gives a feast — needs fish — gatekeeper stops the fisherman — allows to go on the condition of paying half the profit — king asks the price — he begs for 100 lashes — 50 lashes for gatekeeper.*

Once a king arranged a feast. He was fond of fish. Fish was not available. A fisherman brought a fish. The gatekeeper stopped him at the gate. The gatekeeper said. "I can allow you if you give me half of whatever you get". The fisherman agreed. The king was very happy to get the fish. He asked the price of the fish. The fisherman replied, "One hundred lashes on my bare back". The king was shocked. But he ordered for it.

When the fisherman had got fifty lashes, he cried, "Stop, I have a partner in this business. Half of the profit will go to him. It is the gatekeeper". The king understood the story. The gatekeeper got fifty lashes on his bare back. He was dismissed. The fisherman got a good reward.

Moral : *Greed is a curse.*

25. A Cricket and an Ant

Outline : *A cricket lived in a field — spent all its time in singing — lazy — did not store food — the ant — worked day and night — cricket went to ant for food — refused to help.*

Once there was an ant. She lived in a field. A cricket lived near its hole. They were friends. The cricket was lazy. In the months of summer, it sang and made merry. It did not store food for winter. It was careless. The ant was not lazy. She worked day and night. She gathered grains for winter. In winter, the ground was covered with snow. The cricket had nothing to eat. The ant had grains to eat. The cricket went to the ant to borrow some grains. The ant asked it what it had been doing during summer. The cricket replied that it sang and made merry during summer. The ant replied, "If you sang the summer away, you should dance away the winter."

Moral : *No pains, no gains.*

26. The Fox and the Crane

Outline : *A fox and a crane were friends — fox insulted the crane at a dinner — the crane plans to take revenge — crane invited the fox to dinner — served rice in jug — crane enjoyed — fox hungry.*

Once there was a fox. He lived in a jungle. A crane was his best friend. They visited each other's home now and then. One day, the fox invited the crane to dinner. He put the soup in a flat dish. The crane had a long beak. He could not take the soup. The fox licked the dish. The crane felt insulted.

Now the crane wanted to take revenge. He invited the fox to dine with him. He served boiled rice in a jug. Its neck was narrow. The fox could eat nothing. The crane enjoyed the food very much. The fox felt sorry for his behaviour.

Moral : *As you sow, so shall you reap.*

27. The Hen that Laid Golden Eggs

Outline : *A hen laid golden egg daily — the farmer greedy — wishes to become rich overnight — hungry for respect — takes a knife — kills her — finds no eggs — sorry.*

Once, a farmer lived in a village. He was very poor. His income was very small. He passed his days with difficulty. One day, someone gave him a hen. It gave a golden egg everyday. He sold the egg everyday. Soon he became a rich man. All began to respect him in the village. He became greedy. He thought that inside the hen there must be a storehouse of golden eggs. He should get them in a day. Then he would be the richest man in the village. He took a knife and cut the stomach of the hen. He did not get even a single egg. He lost not only the golden eggs but the hen also.

Moral : *Greed is a curse.*

28. The Fox and the Goat

Once a fox was thirsty. Hee roamed here and there and then reached a well. As he stood near the well, he slipped and fell. He could not come out of the well.

By chance a goat reached there. She was also thirsty. She peeped into the well. She found a fox there. The fox said, "Come down sister ! water is fine here." The goat jumped into the well. The fox jumped on her back and with one leap came out of the well. The poor goat was left there. She had to die in the well.

Moral : *Beware of selfish people.*

29. A Foolish Brahmin

Gangu was a brahmin. He was innocent and simple-minded. Once Gangu bought a goat from the fair. He was going back to his home. He met three rogues on the way. They wanted to take the goat from the brahmin. One rogue came to Gangu and said "Why are carrying a dog on your shoulders ? It is very ugly ?" Gangu thought for some time. After some time, he met another rogue. He said "Why are you carrying a sick dog on your shoulders ?" Gangu became doubtful. After some time, the third rogue said," Are you a fool ? Why are you carrying a worthless dog on your shoulders ?" Now the Brahmin became sure that he was not carrying a goat but a dog. He threw down the goat.

Moral : *Do not be too innocent to see through the trick of others.*

30. A Camel and Jackal

Once there lived a camel and a jackal. They were good friends. They lived near a river. One day the jackal came to know that there was a field of ripe melons across the river. His mouth watered. But he could not cross the river. He went to camel and told him about the melons. The camel was also tempted to eat melons. He carried the jackal on his back and crossed the river. Both of them reached the field. They started eating the melons. The jackal started howling loudly. The owner of the field came running and started beating the camel.

When the owner went away the camel asked the jackal why he had howled. The jackal replied, "It is my habit to howl after a heavy meal". Both of them returned to the river. The jackal jumped on the back of the camel. When they were in the middle of the water, the camel began to roll in the water. The jackal said, "Why are you rolling in the water ?" The camel replied, "It is my habit to roll in the water after a heavy meal". The jackal could hardly save himself.

Moral : *Tit for tat.*

31. The Monkey and the Crocodile

There was a tree on which many monkeys lived. In the nearby pond, a pair of crocodiles lived. One day, the female crocodile fell ill. The doctor said that only the heart of a monkey could cure the crocodile. The crocodile offered each of the monkeys to accompany him for a joy ride in the pond. None of them agreed. Lastly, an old monkey agreed. The monkey enjoyed the ride. When they were in deep waters, the crocodile told him his purpose. He said that he wanted the monkey's heart. The monkey said, "Please take me back. I have left my heart on the top of my tree. I can give it to you there". The crocodile took him back to the bank. The monkey went up the tree and disappeared.

Moral : *Presence of mind always works.*

32. A Tailor and the Elephant

Once there lived a tailor in a village. An elephant also lived in the same village. The elephant visited the tailor's shop everyday. The tailor fed him with some thing or the other. They lived like good friends. One day the tailor was not in a good mood. When the elephant came to his shop, he pricked its trunk with a needle. The elephant went to the river and filled his trunk with plenty of mud and dirt. He came running to the tailor's shop. He emptied his trunk all over the tailor and his shop. The tailor was splashed with dirt.

Next day, the tailor asked forgiveness from the elephant and fed him with fresh fruit and vegetables.

Moral : *Do not expect any good in return of bad.*